SOLOMON

SOLOMON

One Dog's Improbable, Two-year,
Thousand-mile Journey to Find Home

Gail Gilmore

Epigraph Books
Rhinebeck, New York

ISBN 978-1-951937-94-2

Library of Congress Control Number 2021900300

Cover design by Ann Kirchner
Book design by Colin Rolfe

Epigraph Books
22 East Market Street
Suite 304
Rhinebeck, NY 12472
(845) 876-4861
epigraphps.com

For Lisa, Ella, and Solomon.
And for all who've taken the long way home.

PART ONE

Underhound Railroad

One

Ears pulled back, tail tucked, the stray dog hides, motionless, behind a tool shed. Like most structures in this Rome, Georgia neighborhood the shed is run-down, its clapboards rotting, its white paint faded and peeling. The dog listens closely, filtering out extraneous sounds, focusing only on the approaching footsteps. Closer and closer they come, and then they stop. There is silence, then a man's voice.

"Hey, boy. C'mon outta there."

The dog detects an edge in the voice. He tenses. He's prepared to run if the man comes closer. But the man doesn't. Instead, he tosses a handful of soft, meaty dog treats off to the side of the shed. The dog smells the food, and his stomach growls painfully. His instincts tell him to run in the opposite direction, away from the man and the food. But his hunger gets the better of him, and he steps out from behind the shed. The man is waiting for him with a long pole. The pole pinches the dog's neck as he's dragged away across patches of dead grass and into a van.

In the Animal Control van the dog struggles to stay upright. He slides back and forth, up and down, his neglected nails scraping the metal floor as the van stops, starts, and turns sharply through the streets. Giving up, he lies down in a corner. The van stops, and the dog rises to a sitting position. When the van's rear doors open he stands, remaining in the corner, as far from the doors as possible. His back literally against the wall, he waits for whatever comes next.

For the first time, he looks at the face of the man who grabbed him with the pole. He sees nothing in the man's expression to put him at ease.

"Alright, easy does it, boy. C'mon over, let's get outta here."

The dog doesn't move.

The man is uneasy. He doesn't want to have to climb in there and haul the dog out. Especially not a cornered dog with ears back and with what looks to be a whole lot of pit bull mixed in with who knows what else. He's going to have to wait this one out, wait 'til the dog's ready. The man sits on the edge of the van, in the middle of the open space, his profile to the dog. He does not make eye contact, doesn't speak. Eventually, seeing the only way out is forward, the dog inches his way toward the van's open door. The man, still silent, tracks the dog's movements with his peripheral vision, then reaches out and slides a slip lead over the dog's head.

"Atta boy. Let's go."

The building is cold, the air conditioning set at high. The chill penetrates the dog's short, black and white fur almost immediately, and he shivers. He's led down a short corridor, then placed in an empty cell. The slam of the grated door closing behind him sets his every nerve on edge. For a moment he stands near the door, watching the man retreat, listening to the frenzied barking of other dogs. Their fear sounds from all directions. He begins to cough. Then, still shivering, he walks to the farthest corner of his cell, lies on the floor, and curls his body tightly into itself. He does not sleep.

Floyd County Animal Control volunteer Ronda Avila uploads the photo of an unusual-looking black and white dog to one of the many "last-chance" sites she regularly uses. The dog in the photo is too thin, and he's clearly miserable. But when Ronda looks at him in person she sees more than neglect and sadness. She sees a tall, handsome dog with a combination of unique markings—a black patch across his side and over his back that resembles a saddle, a black ring around his left eye, black tick marks along the edges of his stand-up ears. She hopes this boy has a taker, because the euthanasia deadline's around the corner.

The Floyd County Animal Control facility in Rome isn't actually a shelter, though Ronda supposes that, technically, it is. If you want to get really literal about it. Which she doesn't. The facility's philosophy has been explained to her clearly by the director, and on many more than one occasion: "This is Animal Control, not a shelter. And that's exactly what I'm doing—controlling animals."

The problem with this interpretation of his professional mandate, Ronda thinks, is that it results in what boils down to wholesale euthanasia. By Georgia law, animals brought into a facility are required to be held for three days. But after that all bets are off. So it doesn't matter if a perfectly adoptable dog or cat has been at Animal Control less than a week, which usually isn't enough time to find the right home or foster situation. No rescue offer by Tuesday? That's it; life over. No reprieve. No second chance.

It seems to Ronda nothing more than arbitrary policy, unrelated to lack of space or to anything else that might make even a lick of sense: Tuesday is the deadline for a rescue offer, Wednesday is euthanasia day. New week, fresh start. Policy. Pure and simple and easy to follow. Especially if you don't really give a damn in the first place. The whole thing is nauseating, but Ronda tries not to dwell on it. If she did, she might just have to quit the place.

And then, to add to an already demoralizing situation, there's the pit bull issue. Floyd County has an ordinance prohibiting the adoption of pit bulls, which in Animal Control practice usually extends to any dog even resembling one. And this black and white dog most definitely does. The law has the unfortunate consequence of making mixed breed dogs like this one unavailable to local residents coming to the facility looking to adopt. Along with the pure pitties, their only chance for survival is an offer of rescue from outside the county. In seven days or less. If the dog is really lucky and arrives at the facility on a Sunday, the seven days might get stretched to nine. Still, even that's a challenge.

For whatever Ronda thinks of the law, which isn't much, it is what it is and she grudgingly operates within its boundaries. But she once worked with someone who didn't. He was an inmate named Philip, who came from the nearby jail to perform daily custodial work at Animal Control. Philip loved the pitties, felt an affinity for them; he knew they most likely wouldn't be getting out alive. Wanting to save those marked dogs, he began hiding them in a large closet on Tuesdays before he left for the day. Then, after all the animals had been euthanized on Wednesday, he'd return the hidden dogs to their cages, hoping they'd appear newly arrived to a less than observant eye. And, for a while, it worked. But eventually the director caught on, Philip was fired, and it was back to business as usual.

Ronda misses Philip, admires his ingenuity and courage. Still, she believes her own best option is to operate creatively within the scope of the law to get animals out of Animal Control as soon as possible. Especially the ones deemed unadoptable by Floyd County. She names the handsome black and white dog Solomon. Giving these dogs a name is important to Ronda. They deserve that dignity, and the name Solomon seems just right for this regal-looking dog. Then she writes what she hopes is a compelling description to accompany his photo, says a silent prayer for him, and hits "post."

Somewhere in New York, a man named Kurt is scrolling through a last-chance rescue site when a photo of a dog named Solomon catches his eye. It's not the best picture. The dog's face is visible only in profile, and the reclining position doesn't provide a true sense of size. But despite the lack of details that usually matter to him in a photo, Kurt finds himself unable to look away.

What holds his gaze has nothing to do with the dog's features. It's the misery, heartbreakingly telegraphed through the dog's posture and facial expression, that pulls him in. Crouched in a cinder-block cage with a grated floor, the dog's body has a coiled quality. It's as if he might bolt right out of there, first chance he gets. But there's also something so deeply sad and hopeless about the dog. The way his chin rests on his paw as if the weight of his head is just too heavy. The way he presses the entire left side of his body, including his face, tightly against the cement blocks.

Kurt isn't really looking for a dog. Not with intention. Still, he's self-aware enough to know he wants one; why else would he be on these sites? But whenever he comes close to making the decision to adopt, he gets cold feet. He worries about the commitment of time, the commitment of money. Sure, it costs a hell of a lot less to raise a dog than it does to raise a kid—something he doubts he'll ever be fully prepared for—but still. Dog food. Supplies. Preventative medications and veterinary care. The expenses all add up.

And if the dog gets sick, things might turn out badly. Veterinary care where he lives is expensive. A friend of his just had to put down the family dog because he couldn't afford the surgery she needed. Or the medication she was going to have to take for the rest of her life. Kurt isn't quite certain he's up to the responsibility of it all.

But this dog Solomon has gotten him good, and he thinks that if there's ever going to be a time to go full-in, it's now. *I'm interested in adopting this dog,* he writes, then hits "send" before he has the chance to second-guess himself.

Back in Rome, Ronda is psyched up. Solomon has gotten an offer of adoption, and in her mind he's as good as out of there. Only problem is, the guy who applied to adopt him lives in New York. In theory, this shouldn't be an issue. But in practice? Different story.

Animal Control volunteers always evaluate potential adopters. If they can't do it themselves, they reach out to their network of volunteers. But that network doesn't stretch as far north as New York. And no matter how desperate she is to get animals out of there as Tuesday approaches, there's no way she's shipping a dog off to just anyone. No. Freakin'. Way.

There's also the transport issue. She can't drive the dog to New York herself, and can't ask anyone else to do that, either. There are two safe, reliable transport services that take dogs up to the Northeast. But no way in hell is Animal Control going to pay for that. What she needs to do is connect with a dog rescue organization based in the New York area. Maybe they can evaluate this guy Kurt and pay for transport.

She researches possible options and decides that Underhound Railroad in Connecticut might be her best bet. They're New England-based, but probably have a volunteer network that could check out an adopter in New York; it's basically right next door. And since they're headquartered in Connecticut, not Georgia, she figures they might have some money to cover transport, too. She picks up the phone.

🐕

Underhound Railroad director Irene Williams doesn't recognize the number on her phone but answers anyway. Probably just the latest in an endless string of annoying telemarketers. Still, she's always afraid if she doesn't answer a call, it'll turn out to be the one time she should have. This caller turns out to be Ronda Avila from Animal Control in Rome, Georgia, requesting assistance from Underhound Railroad for a dog in her facility.

"Yes, absolutely," Irene says. "Happy to help. We'll have someone contact Kurt and schedule a meeting, make sure he's on the up-and-up and has the means to provide for a dog. If he checks out, we'll arrange and pay for the dog's transport."

With that, Ronda feels her anxiety lift, the knot in her shoulders soften.

"Thanks so much. I can't even tell you how much I appreciate it. Next step for him is the vet, and then I'll be back in touch to hammer out details. Thanks again, Irene. For saving his life."

Ronda's next call is to the veterinarian, to confirm the appointment she'd already made on the chance Underhound Railroad was able to help. Now Solomon will have an exam, his shots, the works. Walking back to the dog's cell, she speaks softly to him.

"C'mon, Solomon, time to go see the doctor and get you all squared away. You're gonna have a new life. A good one, this time. I promise."

Solomon is compliant, allowing her to approach and clip the leash onto his collar. They walk out the door, his eyes squinting in the early afternoon brightness, then across the parking lot to Ronda's car. She encourages him to jump into the back seat, and once he's comfortably settled in, she drives the short distance to the vet.

But at the veterinary clinic, everything begins to fall apart. Solomon has heartworm, moderately advanced, and treating it will require an intensive protocol.

"He's going to need medication, and then a month of crate rest. He should really be boarded here for that month. He'll need another month of crate rest after that, but he can do that with his new family," the vet tells Ronda.

None of this is anything Ronda wants to hear. Still, it makes sense. It's October, and given his low body weight he's probably been out all summer living on his own, unprotected from disease-transmitting mosquitoes. Really, she'd like to just smack some people in this world upside the head. Starting with whoever abandoned this dog.

"What's this all going to run?"

"Probably around eight hundred."

Shit, Ronda thinks. Unless the adopter is willing to pay for Solomon's treatment, this story isn't going to have a happy ending.

Underhound Railroad volunteer Connie Rice has connected with Kurt, and is just finishing up his reference check. Finding a time to meet with him on such short notice has proved impossible. For now, a conversation and detailed reference check will have to suffice. Satisfied with what she's learned, she calls Ronda to let her know it's a go. She's not expecting the defeated tone of Ronda's voice.

"I just got back from the vet," Ronda says. "He's got heartworm. Which means he's going to have to stay down here and board at the clinic for a month before he's ready to go. And what with medication and boarding, it's going to cost the adopter about eight hundred bucks."

"Well, that's definitely not great news." Connie sighs. "I'll get back to Kurt with this and see what he says."

She's not hopeful. It can be difficult enough to find homes for healthy dogs. Asking someone to not only adopt a sick dog, but to pay for that dog's medical care? That almost never turns out well. But, every once in a while people surprise her. Maybe this will be one of those times.

"Thanks, Connie. Talk later."

For the next day and a half, Kurt reads and re-reads the e-mails from Underhound Railroad. He feels like a complete shit for not answering them, but knows he'll feel like an even bigger shit if he does. He's gone over it and over it, spun it every which way, but just doesn't see how he can make it work. He doesn't have eight hundred dollars just lying around, and he knows there'll be additional expenses too. Like a large crate. He's gone online to check them out, and they're not cheap.

But beyond the expense of the crate itself, there's the month of crate rest. How is he going to swing that? He's lucky enough to still have his job; a lot of his former co-workers lost theirs when the economy tanked. The pay's not exactly outstanding, but whatever. It's a job. He knows enough about dogs to know you can't leave them locked in a crate all day. And he also knows he can't take a month off of work to stay home so he can take the dog out of the crate for short breaks. Not if he wants to keep his job, anyway.

Still, Kurt can't get the dog out of his mind. The dog's picture is by now so far under his skin that no amount of scratching or picking at facts and reality can dislodge it. His heart reminds him of all the reasons he wants the dog. His mind, in that logical way he finds so irritating, systematically ticks off all the reasons why he can't have what his heart desires. As his mind and heart battle, Kurt feels a kind of paralysis set in, an odd inertia both physical and mental. Unable to allow either side to win, he is ultimately able to do nothing, and leaves every one of Underhound Railroad's e-mails unanswered.

Though disappointed by Kurt's behavior, Irene has to admit she saw it coming. And better to know now that he can't commit to the dog rather than later, after he's already adopted him. With Animal Control's Tuesday deadline looming, Irene does the only thing her conscience will allow. She provides the rescue offer the dog needs. Underhound Railroad will pay for his heartworm treatment and the month of boarding at the vet in Rome, as well as his transport to New England.

Not that Underhound Railroad is flush with discretionary income. Like most rescue organizations, they operate on a shoestring budget. And this dog isn't the kind Underhound Railroad usually rescues. Pittie-looking dogs make some people nervous, can be harder to place. But what's the alternative? Let him die? She'll take her chances on finding him a home. At least she'll be able to sleep at night.

Solomon stands stoically as the woman in this new place runs a gentle hand over his head, his spine. He watches her as she holds something round and shiny between her hands, blowing on it every so often, then placing it against his chest. She smiles at him.

"Good boy, Solomon. Things are sounding better in there."

She leaves after giving him another stroke on his head, and Solomon lies on his bed. He feels stronger, not as tired, and coughs much less. This place is calmer, quieter than the last place he remembers being in.

He's not frightened here. The people he interacts with are kind to him, and he understands they won't hurt him. With each passing day, he feels more like his old self. The self that could run, could walk long distances without coughing and tiring. Life for him in this new place is as good as it's been in a very long time.

While Solomon undergoes his month of crate rest down South, Irene reaches out to her friend and colleague Hope Cruser, who directs Underhound Railroad's operations in Maine, for assistance in finding Solomon a home. Irene posts his picture and story on Underhound Railroad's website, as well as on a few other adoption sites. Neither woman has any luck finding Solomon a forever home. But Hope locates a great foster home for him with a young couple named Steve and Carmen in Kittery, Maine. Steve, an experienced fosterer, is particularly interested in pit bulls and pittie mixes, and the situation seems like a good solution for the next month. In the meantime, the search for a forever home could continue.

Finally, the day arrives for Solomon's transport to his new life. His treatment and first month of crate rest completed, the staff at the veterinary clinic say good-bye to him.

"You be a good boy, Solomon, okay? You're going to have a great home, with people who love you," the vet whispers into his neck as she gives him one last hug.

Then Solomon settles himself into the back seat of a car headed north and begins the first leg of his Underhound Railroad journey.

Two

Solomon is the seventh dog Carmen Fernandez and her boyfriend Steve have fostered together. Many of the dogs on the online "last chance" sites Steve frequents are pitties or pittie mixes. He's passionate about wanting to give them a chance at a good life, mostly because he knows the stats. Pit bulls are not only the most bred dogs, they're the most frequently euthanized. The human irresponsibility inherent in those statistics pisses him off in a big way, deeply offends his morals. So when he came across Solomon's picture online he reached out to Hope. And now here they were on their way to some unfamiliar part of Massachusetts to pick the dog up.

When they arrive at the appointed place, Carmen sees a tall black and white dog. His sturdy body is a little too thin, like the not-quite-filled-out body of an adolescent dog. She knows he's beyond that stage, though, his age estimated at around three years. His low weight is probably a result of the heartworm. But it's not the dog's thinness that stands out to her. What strikes her, and will stick with her for years to come and quite possibly forever, is the unusual and strangely compelling energy surrounding him. He's not a dog, she thinks. He's something else, in the body of a dog.

The thought echoes for a bit in her mind, and in its lingering she realizes what a remarkably odd thought it is. Still, it seems as true as can be to her. The Underhound Railroad volunteer who drove Solomon on the final transport leg to Springfield, Massachusetts and now stands reassuringly beside him tells Carmen and Steve the dog is very skittish. They're used to skittish. Carmen figures that with time, Solomon will be fine. Just like the rest of their foster dogs. The volunteer hands over Solomon's food, treats and a couple of comfort toys to Carmen, while Steve takes hold of Solomon's leash and walks him to the car.

Solomon jumps inside without issue. But once in the back seat, he curls himself into a tight, terrified ball, ears flat against his head, tail tucked. Steve offers him a French fry from a McDonald's bag in the front seat, which he readily accepts and devours. But as soon as the French fry is gone, he assumes his previous position on the seat. Carmen and Steve feel bad for Solomon, but really, it's nothing they haven't seen before. He's just been transported all the way from Georgia. He's had heartworm. And now here he is in an unfamiliar car with two people he's never seen before. I'd be terrified, too, Carmen thinks.

"Poor guy. Maybe he'll perk up a little when we get home and he's got some other dogs to hang out with."

"Yeah, that usually helps," Steve agrees. "He liked that French fry, though—that perked him up for sure!"

"I know, right?" Carmen hopes Solomon is food motivated. It'll make his socialization process much more straightforward.

It's a two-and-a-half hour ride back home to Kittery. Solomon lies motionless on the back seat, and Carmen turns her head to peek at him. She wishes he could relax, let himself fall asleep. He must be exhausted. But every time she glances back he's wide awake, his eyes wary, the expression on his face one she interprets as trepidation.

"It'll be okay, Solomon," she tells him. She hopes he finds the pitch and tone of her voice soothing. "You're going to like living with us."

His ears remain pulled back against his head as Carmen speaks, his body still tightly curled, his tail tucked and invisible. She sighs and turns her head to look out the window at what passes for scenery on the Mass Pike. Within minutes, Solomon begins to whine. He jumps off the seat and onto the floor, hiding behind the driver's seat. From that angle

Carmen can't see him, but before she can release her seat belt to allow herself a full range of vision, she smells it.

"Steve, he just pooped in the car."

"Yup."

"Maybe we shouldn't have given him that French fry. It might've upset his stomach."

"Carmen, it was just one little fry. He's been through a lot in the last twenty-four hours. I'm sure his stomach is upset, but I don't think it's from the fry."

"I guess. Whatever it's from, we need to stop and clean it up."

The next rest area is a few exits ahead, and Steve pulls off the Pike and into the huge parking lot. He finds a quiet space away from the cars and eighteen-wheelers. Carmen gets out and heads to the restroom to grab some paper towels. Steve waits in the car with Solomon, who's once again curled up on the back seat, as far away from the mess as possible, looking miserable.

"It's okay, big guy," Steve tells him. "These things happen. No big deal."

The dog doesn't look like he's buying it, though. Not at all.

Carmen returns carrying two plastic shopping bags from one of the food counters. One bag is empty, the other filled with fistfuls of paper towels—wet, soapy, dry, she has them all. They're going to have to do the clean-up with Solomon in the car. There's no way they're letting him out at a rest stop, even on a leash. He's just too nervous, the possibility of him bolting too great. Steve reaches through the space between the front seats. He clips Solomon's leash to his collar, keeping a tight grip on the leash about a foot away from the dog's body.

"Okay, I've got him. Go ahead and open the door."

Carmen gets into the back seat with Solomon, breathing through her mouth, twisting her body around to avoid stepping in the runny mess. She sops it up with the dry paper towels, goes over the rubber floor mat with the soapy paper towels. Then she deposits it all into the empty plastic bag. Finally, she goes over the area one more time with wet paper towels and blots it with the remaining dry ones.

"We're going to have to clean this again when we get home, with some of that enzyme stuff. But this is okay for now."

The floor mat cleaned, she deposits the plastic bag and paper towels into the nearest trash receptacle. Then they pull back onto the Pike and continue the drive east toward Boston, then north to their home in Kittery, just over the New Hampshire border.

Solomon lies listlessly in his crate, subdued and indifferent. His foster family's dogs prance around the crate's open door, play-posturing, their barks inviting him to come out and join them. But he looks away until the dogs give up on him. Alone, Solomon sighs contentedly. Body warm, belly full, he burrows into the blankets, solitude, and shelter of his crate.

Over the next few weeks, Carmen begins to wonder if Solomon is ever going to adjust to them. He's still on crate rest. They leave the door to his crate open, encouraging him to come out and mingle with them and their dogs. He ventures out a few times to poke his head around the corner, check out what's going on in the next room. Once, he lay down on their bed and allowed Steve to lie next to him. She has the photo to prove it: Steve's hand resting on Solomon's shoulder, his head on Solomon's back, the stiff expression on the dog's face. But mostly, Solomon prefers his crate.

They'd initially worried that keeping Solomon calm for the last month of crate rest might be tough. They'd assumed he'd want to play with their dogs, integrate into the pack. But, sadly, the crate rest part has turned out to be the easiest thing about fostering Solomon. He wants nothing to do with their dogs, and avoids contact whenever he can. He doesn't seem afraid of the dogs, and never displays aggression toward them— or toward her, Steve, or anyone else who comes into the house. But he doesn't show any other kind of emotion, either. Nothing. He seems utterly uninterested in the existence of both dogs and people. She's never seen a dog behave this way. She and Steve discuss the situation with Underhound Railroad. They agree that maybe Solomon just needs more time to get used to his new surroundings. The best thing to do is just wait it out.

And then one day it snows, and everything changes. Carmen and Steve are worried about the snow, Solomon's reaction to it. To the best of their knowledge, it's the first time he's ever seen snow, and they're concerned this unanticipated change in his environment might traumatize him. But when he steps into the yard and onto a blanket of several inches of cold whiteness, his entire demeanor changes. It's a complete 180. He dashes around excitedly, and for the first time since they've brought him home, he wags his tail.

"Oh my God, Steve ... look at him. He's so happy!" Carmen has no idea why this very short-haired dog from the South is so intoxicated with snow. She would've expected just the opposite. Could this, finally, be the unlikely catalyst that activates his emotions?

But once back inside, it's as if his joyful romp through the snow never happened. He immediately heads into his crate, coming out only for meals and to go outside. And once out in the snow again, his tail wags and he races around the yard like the happiest, most normal dog they've ever seen. He even allows one of their dogs to stand up against him, sniff his face. Then back inside, back to ignoring the world around him. It's like flipping a switch. Outside in the snow, emotions on; inside the house, emotions off.

Carmen will later tell Hope that, in retrospect, they shouldn't have been so surprised by what happens a few days later. But they are surprised, and completely unprepared.

Steve and Carmen get new snowboarding equipment for Christmas, and on December 29, they decide to try it out. The snow and the temperature are perfect. Carmen comes home with the familiar exhilaration and exhaustion she always gets from boarding when it's good. She's look-ing forward to unloading the car and then relaxing with a movie for the rest of the afternoon.

They unload the boards first, dumping them inside the front door. The clattering noise of fiberglass on hardwood sends one of their dogs trotting hastily out of the room. Solomon remains in his crate, ignoring them as always, unbothered by the commotion. Carmen wonders if he even notices it. Steve heads back out to the car to collect their remaining equipment, and Carmen meets him halfway, grabs a few things from his overloaded hands. As they open the front door, everything is as ordinary as breathing. Until it's not. Until Solomon shoots out of his crate, pushes them aside with his large, strong head, and takes off up the street.

For the first seconds after Solomon's escape, Steve and Carmen are shocked into paralysis. Then Steve is out the door in pursuit. He can see Solomon at the top of the street. *Damn.* Why couldn't he have run in the opposite direction, where their quiet street dead-ends down by the water? Instead, he's at the other end, the end that intersects with one of the most heavily traveled roads in town. They need to get him before he tries to cross the street.

"Solomon! Hey, boy … c'mon back," Steve calls. He knows the dog can see him, can hear his voice. But Solomon remains where he is. Steve starts to panic. This has never happened to him, and he's not sure what to do. The only thing he can think of is food. He sprints back to the house and grabs a can of dog food and a plastic container of kibble, then races back out. Carmen follows him, stomach churning, brain numb. Solomon watches them approach, but makes no move until Steve throws a handful of kibble up the street. Once the dog smells the food, he walks toward them, eating the kibble as he goes. Steve pops open a can of dog food, tosses it up the street to where Solomon stands.

"He's not too far away," Steve says. "It'll take him a few minutes to eat that; we should be able to just walk up and grab him."

But every time Steve and Carmen approach Solomon he takes off, returning to his can of food only when they retreat. Finally, the can is empty. He runs back to the end of their street, dashes across the busy intersection, and disappears into the winter dusk.

They put off calling Hope for as long as they can.

"Why didn't you grab him when he ran out the door?" Steve demands.

"Well for one thing, I didn't have a free hand. And for another, it happened so fast, I barely saw him run past us."

"You still could've grabbed him."

"Don't blame me, Steve. Why didn't *you* grab him?"

Steve says nothing.

"It's not our fault," Carmen continues. "No one could've predicted this."

"It's not our fault? Well whose fault is it, then? It happened on our watch, Carmen. What am I supposed to tell Hope? That we lost the dog she trusted us to foster?"

"I don't know, Steve." She hates it when he gets like this. "But maybe instead of standing here arguing, we should go out and look for him?"

They spend hours driving around the neighborhood, knocking on doors, asking if anyone has seen a large black and white dog with cow-like markings. A few people say yes, sending the two speeding off in the latest direction Solomon might be heading. But they turn up no sign of him. It's as if he's completely vanished. As darkness closes in, it's clear they're going to have to notify Hope that Solomon has gone missing.

Hope is in Rhode Island visiting family for the holidays. When she gets Steve's frantic call she leaves immediately for Maine. Sick with worry, she exceeds the already generous speed limit by twenty miles an hour along every stretch of open highway from Rhode Island to southern Maine. Solomon has just finished his second month of crate rest—he should absolutely not be running around outside in the frigid Maine winter. They need to find him. Fast.

Hope lives two hours north of Kittery, in Boothbay Harbor, but stops in Kittery on her way home. She wants to get the full story from Steve and Carmen, and to try to calm Steve down. Inside, she's a frantic, emotional mess, but it's not going to help if everyone loses it at the same time. Someone needs to remain calm, at least outwardly. The three of them devise a short-term plan. Hope will go home to Boothbay that night, put together and print up a flyer. She'll get it copied in the morning, and return to Kittery so the three of them can flyer the area. In the meantime, Steve and Carmen will continue to drive around Kittery looking for Solomon, and will notify local police and veterinary offices that he's missing.

The next day Hope is back in Kittery, armed with a stack of 250 flyers in plastic sleeves. Planning to stay in Kittery until Solomon is found, she checks into a motel, then heads over to pick up Steve and Carmen at their house. The three of them drive around town, putting up the flyers with Solomon's picture and Steve's and Hope's phone numbers anywhere they can. They stop at stores, ask if they can hang the flyer in a window or on a corkboard. LOST, the flyer says. SHY. DO NOT CHASE! Solomon is in flight mode now, and Hope prays that whoever sees him will follow this directive. If not, he could be spooked from the area. Or worse.

Before calling it quits for the day, they put up all 250 flyers. They leave dog blankets and unwashed clothes heavy with Steve's scent outside in the areas where Solomon was seen the first day he went missing. When Hope turns out the lights in her motel room that night, she has no reason to believe they won't find Solomon, won't be able to recover him. Tomorrow, maybe. Or the day after that. But by the end of the week, for sure.

That night, Solomon finds a shed in the yard of a house next to a cemetery and hunkers down beneath it. He curls up, his body generating heat. Even so, the cold seeps in. When the sun rises enough to warm, he wiggles his way out, shakes the dirt from his body, and heads for the cemetery. In the far corner, near the woods, he finds a gravestone standing in a large splash of warm sunlight. He lowers his body to the ground, his back against the stone, and falls asleep.

In the late afternoon, he returns to his spot under the shed. He tries to sleep, but his stomach comes alive with a familiar ache and he leaves the shelter of the shed in search of food. He prowls the neighborhood streets, rooting through trash barrels and dumpsters, but finds little of value to a hungry dog. He returns to the shed, and the next morning heads again to the cemetery. This becomes his new routine. As he settles in and becomes more familiar with his surroundings, he takes more risks. Driven by the relentless gnawing in his stomach, he travels the area in wider circles, searching for a reliable source of food.

One night, he finds what he's been searching for. At the edge of a parking lot, behind a retirement community complex near the highway, is a dumpster with accessible food. But the area has no sheds or other structures for him to shelter under. Stomach full, he walks into the shallow woods behind the complex and digs himself a nest in the snow. For the first time in many nights, he sleeps soundly.

While Hope obsessively checks Google Earth for bodies of water, shallow wooded areas near houses, cemeteries, and other places a missing dog might be drawn to, Steve begins tracking Solomon. They get a call from a man living in a house bordering the Oak Grove Cemetery. The man says he's seen Solomon several times, cutting across his yard, heading to and from the cemetery.

Steve drives over to take a look around. The area seems a likely place for a dog on the run to hide out. The caller's yard contains lots of overgrown brush. Out back and off to the side of the house are a couple of out-buildings that have seen better days. Multiple places to tuck into, or under, for shelter. And, just as the caller said, there's a direct route through the yard into the cemetery.

The cemetery itself is bordered by woods, giving Solomon a perfect escape route should he need it. The narrow roads and narrower pathways through the headstones provide multiple entry and exit points. Some of the headstones rest atop small inclines, lending both a broad vantage point and safety. Lying with his back against a headstone, Solomon wouldn't feel vulnerable to a person or animal sneaking up on him from behind. The cemetery is open and sunny, making it an ideal place for a cold dog to warm up on a day when the sun's shining.

As Steve walks along the pathways looking for dog prints in the snow, he inhales the moist scent of pine, absorbs the deep quiet of this infrequently visited place. A Maine cemetery in winter; what a perfect resting spot for a dog trying not to be found. He stills himself for a moment in the peacefulness of it. Birds singing, birches starkly white against the winter blue sky. If you were a dog, he asks himself, where would you go? As he continues to observe his surroundings, he notices that the right side of the cemetery is hilly, more wooded. He figures that would be the area most likely to attract Solomon.

It's not long before Steve finds what he's looking for—prints in the snow. Dog or coyote? He squats down, takes a closer look. No clear X between the pads. On the front set of prints, prominent claw marks on each pad. More wide than oblong. Dog. Definitely dog. He follows the tracks into the shallow woods. But once under the canopy, he sees that further tracking is pointless. The large clumps of heavy, melting snow falling from the upper branches of the evergreens have either obliterated or altered the prints. Besides, what would he do if he sees Solomon? It's not like the dog is going to willingly come to him. *That*, he reminds himself, is a proven fact. At this point, he figures the best thing to do is go home, call Hope, and come up with a more long-range plan.

The plan they devise to recover Solomon is comprehensive, with moving parts meant to cover all possibilities. They set food at the cemetery, and a trap that Hope's boyfriend builds. For a week, Hope, Steve, and

Carmen take turns checking the trap throughout the night. Carmen and Steve get up at three o'clock in the morning and drive around Kittery for hours in the darkness, looking for Solomon. Nothing. The sighting calls stop coming, too. At this point, the dog seems to have disappeared not only from the Oak Grove cemetery area, but from the planet.

"He's onto us," Hope tells Carmen and Steve. "He's definitely onto us."

Maybe, Carmen thinks. But she also has her own theory, one she keeps to herself. She strongly believes that Solomon, for reasons she doesn't understand, had wanted out of their home since the day he came to live with them. He finally saw his chance and took it. Onto them or not, he won't be coming back.

Hope creates a Facebook page, Help-us-find-Solomon, hoping it might generate some calls. She's convinced people are seeing him; with his unusual markings he's kind of hard to miss. But unless they happen to see a flyer, they're not going to know he's missing, or have a number to call. So Hope has a huge road sign made, with Solomon's picture, the word MISSING, and the phone numbers to call if he's seen. Down near the Kittery exit off Route 95 there's a crazy knot of roads, and this is where she places the sign. Before long, they have more sightings than they can keep up with.

"There's a big black and white dog out back, out by the trucks. Seen him just this morning, matter of fact. Think he might be living in the woods or something," a resident of the retirement community tells another resident.

"Why would a dog be out back there? Probably a coyote. You sure it's a dog?"

"Yup. Seen him more than once. Got a collar on."

"Well you oughta probably tell someone, then."

So he tells one staff member, and then another, and another. But no one believes him. Not until one of those staff members sees the newly erected road sign with the picture of a missing black and white dog. The retirement community's director contacts a Maine Guide and asks him to check out the property's back area for signs of the dog. The request doesn't fall within the purview of a Guide's typical work—accompanying hikers, rafters, hunters, snowmobilers, and campers while in or on Maine's forests or waters—but he agrees to come over and take a look. The Guide finds an animal nest up behind the garages in back of the property, just a little bit into the woods. It's dug into the snow, with some leaves on the bottom. On close examination he observes black and white hairs in the leaves and snow. The prints around the nest are clearly a dog's.

The discovery of Solomon's nest is the beginning of the next big push to recover him. His location, though now at least known, is highly problematic. The retirement community is dangerously close to busy Route 95. Once he settles in up there he begins traveling back and forth across the highway, creating chaos for motorists. On one particular day, the Maine State Police receive sixteen calls in one hour about Solomon.

"He's sitting on that little delta, between the exits to 95 North and South," one caller reports.

"A big black and white dog just ran across the highway. Please go get him before he gets killed!" implores another.

"There's a black and white dog running along the highway."

The police respond immediately, notifying Hope while en route to Solomon's location. Hope calls for some back-up volunteer assistance, and when she arrives the police and a few volunteers have Solomon cornered on the delta. A plan is thrown together. The volunteers and police circle Solomon, moving in closer and closer, tightening the circle until they're close enough for someone to grab him. We've got him, Hope thinks. Finally. But as the woman closest to Solomon reaches out to grab his collar, he slips right through her legs. Devastated, the group watches as he bolts across the highway and into the woods. They will never again be that close.

The most surprising thing after the episode on the delta is that Solomon remains in the area. He's still being seen everywhere. Crossing Route 95 into Eliot, the next town over from Kittery. Walking along the Piscataqua River. Passing by houses bordering the Piscataqua. Hope gets frequent calls from people who see him in riverside neighborhoods. A videographer takes a video of Solomon killing ducks and forwards it to Hope. In the video, Solomon grabs a duck, shakes it, eats part of it, tosses it aside, grabs another one, flings it into the air.

On the one hand, Hope finds the footage horrifying. On the other hand, she's encouraged by Solomon's resourcefulness, impressed by his survival skills. The longer he can survive on his own, the more time that buys to recover him. The sightings in Eliot go on for a while. Eventually, a trap is set on the property of the videographer; a trap Solomon never goes into. Instead, he continues his travels back and forth across Route 95, and up and down the street parallel to the delta and highway.

Hope discovers that if she drives the loop by the delta and the highway long enough, she'll see Solomon. At the moment, she tracks him in her car. She always seems to be on the wrong side of the road. Or just a few feet behind or ahead of him. It's making her crazy. It just never fails: if he's on one side of the road, by the time she turns around and gets to that side, he's on the other. And he's running. Which freaks her out more than anything else, because he absolutely should not be running. But he is. Right behind her car. She keeps an eye on him in the rearview mirror as he veers off the road and crosses behind her to the other side. Hope hears the crash before she sees the car she rear-ends.

After the accident Hope returns to Boothbay. Staying in Kittery isn't an option without a car, so while her car's in the shop she does what she can from home. She updates Solomon's Facebook page to keep people aware and looking for him. She calls the shelters every few days to see if anyone has brought him in. She even consults a psychic. Nothing comes of any of it. By mid-February the sighting calls stop. They have absolutely no idea where he is.

Solomon is on edge. He's been feeling wary ever since he returned to his nest in the snow to find the scent of humans all around it. He remains at his home base behind the retirement complex. But he's hypervigilant now, ears constantly turned out to catch unfamiliar sounds, nose repeatedly searching the air for human scents. He knows people are trying to catch him, and he's spooked. Often out of breath from running, from hunting flying animals on the ice, he senses his vulnerability.

One night in February, he doesn't return to his nest. Instead, with nothing to guide him but the moon and his instincts, he leaves the area quickly, quietly. He travels west for days until, finding a narrow, frozen section of the Piscataqua River, he crosses into New Hampshire, heading south.

When Solomon sets off on the first solo leg of his journey into the unknown, he has no idea of the dangers facing him. Underhound Railroad's volunteers and Solomon's foster family do.

Of all the things that could happen to Solomon, the most pressing concern for Hope is his recent heartworm treatment. It's still too soon for his six-month check-up to determine if the heartworms have been completely eliminated. She doesn't know how compromised his heart and lungs may be. But she does know that when heartworms begin to die, they break into pieces that can block pulmonary vessels. This is most likely to happen when dogs are allowed too much exercise following treatment, and is the main reason dogs die post-treatment. Solomon's been running all over Kittery, in extreme cold temperatures, for weeks. The thought of it keeps her awake long into most nights.

There are other dangers, too. She ticks them off on a mental list:

Frostbite on his ears, nose, tail, and pads;

Falling through the ice on a pond or river and drowning;

Getting into an altercation with wild animals;

No reliable source of food and water, which increases the possibility of eating roadkill that can transmit diseases like roundworm or contain rodenticide; and

Being struck, injured, and possibly killed by a vehicle while crossing a street or highway.

Had Hope known Solomon was making his way steadily south and then southwest, defying the odds of survival with every passing day, she might've worried less, slept more. Then again, probably not.

Three

For the next six weeks Solomon is on the move. He travels at night, unseen, searching for food, his continual movement keeping his body warm through the frigid nighttime temperatures. The sun is warmer now. On sunny days he finds out-of-the-way places to bake the cold out of his body, to sleep. Unlike in Kittery, he doesn't settle in anywhere; when darkness arrives and the temperature falls, he's usually up and gone.

At some point in February, Solomon finds his way to the Merrimack River. This convenient source of water is a boon. When he's unable to find or hunt food, drinking water temporarily eases the pain in his belly. And so he follows the river in a south/southwesterly direction, eventually crossing the border into Massachusetts.

One early morning, as the sun begins to rise, he comes across a chain link fence. Drawn to its linear structure, he walks alongside it for a time before arriving at a damaged section of fencing. He tilts his head to the side, examining the opening, then squeezes his body through it. He has no idea what's on the other side of the fence, but he's looking for an easy, accessible food source.

Instead, what he finds after a quick dash up a small incline is a large, quiet area of field and woods. He trots across the field and into the woods, where he discovers a small, shallow cave created by the space beneath the branches of a fallen evergreen tree. Cautiously sniffing around its perimeter for the scent of other animals, he finds none. He crawls inside. Layers of dead leaves and pine needles line the bottom of the cave, and he digs at them until the nest he forms is to his liking. He lies down, curls up, and falls into a deep sleep.

He remains in this place with its cozy cave for weeks. It's comfortable, safe, and secluded. One day, his stomach pinching and rumbling, he discovers there's also food. He sees a small animal, and his instincts kick in. Chasing after the animal, he finds it doesn't run nearly as fast as he does. He easily overpowers and kills it with a quick snap of its neck. Now aware of the existence of these animals he begins actively hunting them, and for the first time since leaving his foster home, he has a reliable food source.

But Solomon's anonymity and freedom to roam unseen don't last. Unbeknownst to him, he's living on the property of a waste-to-energy facility in Haverhill, Massachusetts called Covanta, and when two of the facility's employees come across him, their discovery sets in motion a series of events that will alter the trajectory of his journey.

No one at Covanta remembers exactly when. But sometime in March 2011, a large black and white dog with markings like a Holstein is spotted in a remote section of the 70-acre tract sprawled along the Merrimack River. The property is hilly, with woods and small fields. With the exception of the main facilities area, it's very quiet. Employees have seen ducks, deer, hawks, woodchucks, raccoons, and the occasional coyote. But this is the first time anyone can recall seeing a lone dog.

Bob Spinney and his colleague Red chuckle about it. Probably a local dog gone temporarily AWOL. He'll eventually get hungry and go on back home. The fact that the dog is wearing a collar bolsters this theory, and they're not expecting to see him again. But a couple of weeks later, on a drive through the property, they come across him hanging out in a little-used area behind the landfill. Surprised, Bob stops the SUV. He and Red get out and approach the dog, who watches them, motionless, until they're within twenty-five feet. And then he bolts, disappearing into the woods.

"Does he look kinda skinny to you?" Red asks. "He looks skinny to me."

"Looks skinny to me, too."

"Wonder if he's okay. It's strange that he's still hanging around here. Maybe we oughta put some food out for him."

"Yeah. No idea how he wound up here, but if he has a home, he hasn't gone back to it. Poor guy…" Bob shakes his head. If there's one thing he can't stand, it's seeing an animal suffer. That afternoon, on his way home, he stops at the local BJ's and buys dog food and a few industrial-size boxes of dog treats. No way is that dog going hungry out there. Not if he has something to say about it.

The dog stays mostly out of sight, avoiding the main facilities area. Too much noise, Bob supposes. But out-of-sight doesn't equal out-of-mind, not to Bob and Red. They worry about the short-haired dog out there in the elements. Winter isn't over in Massachusetts until April, some years not even then. So the men build him a lean-to adjacent to the basin, a quiet, grassy area near the Leach A building. This, they agree, will be the best place for his shelter. Easily accessible for them, but sufficiently out of the way for him.

During the week, Bob or Red puts out food and water for the dog, and on weekends Covanta's accountant Wendy takes care of replenishing it. Sometimes Wendy sits in her car afterward, hoping to see the dog head over to the lean-to for his meal. There's something about him, about his situation, that really gets to her. He has all his basic survival needs met, she reminds herself. But still. He doesn't have what she believes every dog needs. A home, a family. And that's the thing that shreds her heart.

By the time spring's trees have leafed out, the dog has visibly fattened up. And the Covanta staff has given him a name: Bud. Bud, now more comfortable with his surroundings, frequently hangs out on the hill opposite the offices, keeping an eye on the trucks rolling in and out. Sometimes he observes the mowing of the lawn. If he's not sitting up on the hill, he's running around the property chasing animals. Red also sees him down at the river every once in a while. The area of the Covanta property that runs along the Merrimack is fenced. But long years and inclement weather have caused sections of the chain link to give way, leaving gaps wide enough for Bud to squeeze through. When the weather gets hot he heads down to the river and slips through the fencing to take a dip. Then he goes back to the hill to dry off in the sun.

The whole place, Bob thinks, is like a huge playground for dogs. In the summer months, when he's driving his SUV through the more remote areas of the property, he sees Bud chasing deer and killing woodchucks. He doesn't need to kill woodchucks for food; God knows, he has plenty of food and treats. All he has to do to get them is saunter on over to his lean-to. He must be grabbing them, shaking them, and flinging them around just for the fun of it.

"No toys, so the woodchucks have to fill in, I guess," he tells Red.

"I guess. I feel bad for the woodchucks, but no way we're gonna be able to stop him from doing it. I just hope I don't have to see it."

When October arrives, Red leaves the garage door in the Leach A building raised partway. It's just enough for Bud to be able to get inside out of the chilly night air. Even with the door raised, the temperature inside the garage remains a consistent sixty to sixty-five degrees. It's a perfect fall and winter shelter. Wendy brings an old feather-filled duvet to the garage and makes a bed for Bud, and Bob moves the dog's food and water from the lean-to into the garage.

Things are just about perfect for Bud at Covanta. But then, in late October, some suit gets nervous about having a stray dog on the property. Bob's and Red's boss, a fan of Bud's, struggles to keep his own feelings below the surface as he explains the issue.

"He thinks having Bud on the property could be a liability. You know, that someone might inadvertently sneak up on him and startle him, get bitten, and then sue. I guess we're going to have to call Animal Control or the Animal Rescue League and see if they can catch him."

It falls to Red to make these calls. The whole thing seems unnecessary, completely preposterous. Christ, the dog wouldn't let you get within twenty-five feet of him. And no way is anyone sneaking up on him and surprising him. That dog could hear a pin drop on velvet. Still, the complaint comes from further up the food chain; not much he can do about it. He makes the calls, and is eventually connected with Lori Bertrand, a Granite State Dog Recovery (GSDR) Board member and volunteer who lives right up the street on the Massachusetts–New Hampshire line.

The story Red tells Lori about a dog named Bud isn't the kind of missing dog report she typically hears from callers reaching out to GSDR. Usually a caller's dog is missing from an unfenced yard, or because of fireworks or thunderstorms. Or, occasionally, after chasing wildlife while walking off-leash in the woods. And the longest case she's ever worked was a dog missing for a few months. This is the first time she's heard of a dog camping out for eight months in one place. She also finds it interesting that no one has contacted GSDR, the Haverhill Animal Control Officer (ACO), or local police about a missing dog resembling the one Red describes. She's already checked. Probably dealing with an abandoned dog, she thinks. With no owner, they'll need to find him a placement before they recover him. It's always the trickiest part of working with this category of dog. But they'll figure things out. They always do.

"Sure," she tells Red. "I'm happy to come over, take a look around, set up some equipment and get the ball rolling."

"That'd be great."

Lori hears the hesitation in his voice, the way the tone doesn't quite match the words. "Are you familiar with how we work?" she asks.

"No, not really."

"Okay, I'll give you a very brief rundown. The first thing we always do is set up a camera. We want to see the dog, observe his behavior. Then we set a feeding station, but we won't need to do that with Bud since he already has one. With him, we'll just get the camera up, and since we already know his location and routine, probably move right to the trapping phase."

Red is silent.

"We use humane traps. There's no way he's going to get hurt."

"Good to know."

She hears in his half-there smile that he wishes things were different, wishes Bud could stay at Covanta.

"You guys have been so great to him, Red. He couldn't have landed in a better place, with more caring people. You probably saved his life."

"Wouldn't have had it any other way."

Lori drives over to Covanta with a trail camera. She sets it up on a yellow pole in the Leach A garage, lens pointed at Bud's food and water bowls. When she returns the next day, she pulls the SD card from the camera and replaces it with a new one. Once home, she pops the pulled card into her laptop. The dog that appears on her screen looks like no dog she's ever seen. He's clearly a mixed breed, but she has no idea what that mix consists of. Pit bull? Cattle dog? Great Dane? Some or none of the above? She'll have to send the pictures to fellow GSDR Board member and volunteer Beth Corr for identification. If anyone's ever seen this type of dog before, it's Beth.

To Lori, the dog is stunning. And it's more than just his physical beauty. There's something in the way he carries himself, something in his expression that conveys a deep wisdom. Something that draws her to him. Scary smart, she thinks. This dog is scary smart. She may not know the dog's breed, or anything else about him, but there's one thing she does know. It'd be easier to get the proverbial camel through the eye of a needle than it's going to be to get this dog through the door of a trap. They were in for it with this one.

When Beth gets the pictures from Lori, she immediately thinks cattle dog and pit bull, with maybe a bit of Texas Heeler. Still, she wouldn't put money on it. None of them have ever seen a dog that looks anything like him. And they don't have the usual owner's description to clue them in. Just the pictures from the trail cam. He looks to be in pretty good shape; no visible ribs, no external injuries. His collar seems a little tight, though, which makes her think he may have been out for quite a while. But the most vivid, striking thing about those pictures, the thing that sticks with her and won't let go, is this: from the moment she sees his face, she knows she's going to be involved in recovering him. Or in whatever his journey turns out to be. It's like an instant soul connection. Not definable, not explainable. Just *known*.

A few days later, Lori and Beth are on their way to Covanta with the trap. The Animal Rescue League has agreed to take Bud in at the ARL Boston shelter, work with him on socialization. They're all set. Now they just need to get the dog into the trap and he'll be on his way to a new life, one that will include a loving family. They place the trap right outside the Leach A garage. The camera on the pole inside the garage provides a clear shot at the goings on around the trap from beneath the raised door. Then they set his food, and wait.

Beth sits in front of her computer, scrolling through the pictures of Bud from the trail cam. Frame by frame, she analyzes his behavior as he approaches the trap. His food, initially placed outside the trap to help him associate the metal box with something positive, now sits inside it, just beyond the raised trip plate. He's shown no previous signs of nervousness over the trap, no hesitation to eat the food set next to it. But he refuses to enter it. In one frame he stands in front of the trap, looking into it warily, seeing no exit from the other end. If this were a comic strip, Beth thinks, his thought bubble would read "Do you *really* think I don't know this is a trap? LMAO!!"

"He's never going in there," Beth says aloud to herself. "Not in a

million years." Lori was right; tougher than a camel through the eye of a
needle. They need a different kind of trap. Something with a large, open,
electromagnetic door. To the best of her knowledge, though, there's
nothing like that out there. If she wants it, she's going to have to build
it herself.

After days of internet research, Beth draws up a plan for an electromagnetic, marine battery-operated trap. Her plan looks good in theory.
Still, she knows nothing about electricity, or if the plan she's sketched
out is even feasible. What she needs is an electrical engineer. She posts
a request on Facebook, and through mutual friends is referred to Joe,
a retired electrical engineer living in southeastern Massachusetts. She
scans and e-mails her drawing to him, and is ecstatic when she gets his
reply: Yes, it's doable.

Beth orders an electromagnet; a pull-up, pressure-proof lock; and
some self-closing hinges on Amazon. She purchases a marine battery
at a local store and drives to a nearby electrical supply company to ask
about switches.

"I'm looking for a two-piece switch that completes a circuit, but kills
the circuit when the pieces aren't together. Do you have anything like
that here?"

"We do have something like that. It's a switch that automatically
turns on a closet light when someone opens the door, and turns the light
off when the door gets closed. But it's not exclusive to closets; you can
use it for other things, too."

"Could I use it for a trap?"

"A trap? What exactly do you mean by a trap?"

While Beth tells him about Bud, and the trap she and Joe are design-
ing and building, the man's expression morphs from suspicion to relief.

"Sure. This kind of switch would work for that."

"Wonderful. Sold!"

Back at home, Beth sits at her laptop and types a list of things she's ordered and purchased. A while back someone had donated a large kennel to GSDR. She's sure she can borrow it, and adds it to her list. Then she e-mails the list to Joe, who gets to work on drawing up the schematic.

On a Friday night in late November, Joe battles the rush hour traffic and drives up to Haverhill from his home in Taunton. In his car are the schematic, along with the physical components of the new trap. He and Beth call it the Gypsy trap, in honor of the always-on-the-move dog they hope to recover in it. Beth meets Joe at Covanta with the electrical equipment and a freshly charged marine battery. Everything is set to go. The goal is to assemble the Gypsy trap that night at Covanta and show Red and Bob how to operate it. There's no plan to make it live that night. They want to see how Bud reacts to it, give him time to get accustomed to its presence.

They connect the pieces of the Gypsy trap inside the Leach A garage, then place it outside, in the same location as the first trap. But Bud won't go anywhere near it. Beth is devastated. She'd been confident that the trap's openness would do the trick; clearly, this is not the case. Wondering if a change of location might help, she enlists Bob and Red to help move the trap into the Leach A garage. They position the trap with its front end open and flush against the garage door. Red and Bob suggest using a sign stored in the garage to block out some of the light coming into the garage from under the lifted door. With the sign in place, the entrance area and the garage as a whole are darker.

"Great idea, guys," Beth says. "The trap's not nearly as obvious now. Just kind of blends into the darkness."

The trap measures three and a half by ten feet, but Bud can't see it from a distance the way he could when it was set up outside. There's no advance warning; it's right there, as soon as he enters the garage. Beth hopes it'll seem like less of an object to him and more a kind of extension of the opening to the garage. Satisfied with the new set-up, they put Bud's food beside the trap and begin the waiting process all over again.

One day in late December, Bob is on his way to lunch. As he passes the Leach A building, he hears the faint sound of metal on metal. Could it be the trap door closing? He ducks into the garage and there's Bud, standing quietly in the trap. It breaks Bob's heart to see the dog standing there, gazing out at him with an expression he can't quite read. He's never seen Bud close up, and now has the opportunity to take in the details of his face, the intricacies of his markings. Damn. The dog's a beauty. There's a small part of him that wants to open the trap, let Bud out. But his stronger, better self wants Bud to have the home he deserves.

He reaches tentative fingers through the trap's grid, runs them gently over the dog's head.

"I'm sorry, Bud. We're gonna miss you here, boy. But there's a better life for you out there, a family waiting to give you lots of love. And that's how it should be."

He turns and walks out of the garage, the lump in his throat tight, and calls the Animal Rescue League.

Less than two hours later Solomon once again finds himself in a van, this time secured in a large crate facing the vehicle's back doors. The man's voice coming from behind him is quiet and steady. Still, he pants loudly, his heart racing.

The van stops and the back doors open. A slip lead is placed over his head, and he's taken out of the crate and led a short distance into a building. The sounds of barking surround him, and his sensory memory of the building in Georgia kicks in. Walking down a corridor with the man, he tucks his tail tight against his belly.

He soon learns this place is different. Here he has a bed, and people spend time with him both in and outside his run. He stands quietly while they pet him, and trots obediently beside them when he's taken for short walks to relieve himself. But when left to his own devices, he retreats to the far end of his run, ignores people passing by, refuses food.

Solomon doesn't know he's at Boston's Animal Rescue League shelter. Or that his continued withdrawn, depressed affect is concerning to the League's Director of the Center for Animal Protection, Lieutenant Alan Borgal. Alan consults a few animal behavior specialists. Their consensus is that the prognosis for the dog's successful socialization is poor enough that he might have to be euthanized. But Alan is nowhere near ready to give up. He decides to get the dog, who the ARL has named Rugby, out of the shelter for a while.

He calls former colleague Sheila D'Arpino, a veterinarian specializing in shelter dog behavior. Alan explains the situation with Rugby; the dog's inability to connect with the staff, his prognosis for socialization.

"Honestly, I think you may be his last best chance," Alan tells Sheila.

"What do you know about him?" Sheila asks.

"Not much. He was trapped up in Haverhill, at Covanta. Been living there at the facility for nine, ten months. Seems to be an abandoned dog; no one's reported him missing that we know of. No chip, either. Only thing I know for sure is that he's not doing well here. I think he needs to get out of the shelter environment, ASAP. He's going to be a real challenge, this one."

"Well, you know me. The more of a challenge, the better. Bring him over whenever you want."

"How 'bout today?"

"Today's fine."

Before long, Solomon finds himself back on the road in the Animal Rescue League van, heading southwest into the unknown.

Four

The dog lies on a bed in a refurbished shed, food and water bowls nearby. The quiet and solitude of his environment is a welcome change from the place he just left. The silence is abruptly broken by footsteps on the winter-hardened ground outside the shed. He lifts his head and turns his ears outward, listening, wary. As the shed door opens, he lowers his head back onto his front paws and waits for whatever comes next.

Sheila D'Arpino leans against the door frame of the small, cozy, shed-like building in her backyard, observing the dog quietly, careful not to make eye contact. He's exactly where she left him after they returned from his morning walk several hours earlier. Same position, too: lying on his bed, body stretched alongside the wall, head resting on his paws.

She's worked with many dogs like Rugby in the little shed. The D'Arpino property is five acres, and includes a large fenced-in yard. She considers the place a kind of halfway house for dogs with histories of fearful, shut-down behavior. A stress-free, quiet place where a dog can be exposed to people and other dogs in small doses, building up his comfort level. Sort of like exposure therapy, but for dogs.

The dog watches her approach. He doesn't shy away, or growl at the leash in her hand. Either behavior would be understandable; he's been with her for just a week and a half, and socialization takes time. What she doesn't understand is his lack of reaction toward her. Though she's only inches away, he doesn't even look up. It's as if she doesn't exist to him. The dog's flat affect and emotionless attitude is a new experience for her. He reminds her of a canine zombie, and her heart aches for him.

Sheila bends down and pets his head, something he's allowed her to do from the beginning. The slight flinch beneath her hand tells her he endures more than enjoys her touch. But human touch is good for his socialization, so as long as he continues to allow it, she'll continue to do it.

"Good boy," she tells him, hooking the leash to his collar. There's something about the sound of the metal clip hooking onto his collar that bothers him. He immediately pulls his ears back, flat and tight against his head. It's odd, Sheila thinks; though he obviously dislikes the process of being leashed, he seems to her happiest when he's outside. It's a muted sort of happiness, though: tail untucked, ears up; the typical signs of neutral body language in a dog as opposed to the way most dogs express joy. But for Rugby they indicate as much happiness as he appears capable of—at least for now.

"C'mon, Rugby, let's go outside." When he doesn't move, she tugs the leash gently upward. With that the dog rises and walks along beside her, out the door and into the fenced-in yard. When he first came to live with her and her husband, Pete, Sheila walked Rugby by himself. But after a week of solo walks she introduced him to her dogs, hoping to get the socialization process moving forward. And it *is* moving, she thinks. Just very slowly.

It's going well in that he doesn't challenge the pack order at all, but not so well in terms of him connecting with the other dogs. Forging these canine relationships is important to a dog's socialization. Yet he continues to show as much interest in them as he does in her and Pete. Which is exactly zero. He's already had his pack walk this morning, so she decides to take him out alone for his afternoon walk. Maybe he'll be a little happier by himself.

He's surprisingly well-mannered on leash. Sheila thinks it's possible Rugby was previously trained. It's more likely, though, that his docile behavior on leash has more to do with his general lack of enthusiastic connection to everything and everyone. If this dog could talk, she thinks, he'd probably just look at her and say "Meh. Whatever…"

They walk across the yard and through the gate, Sheila's breath visible in the cold air. Then, out to the street and down the sidewalk, all of it by now familiar to Rugby. Sheila watches for signs of engagement with something. *Any*thing. He sniffs, desultorily, at the occasional scent, but nothing more.

At the half-mile mark they turn around and head home. Back through the gate, back across the yard, back into the cozy shed. She unhooks his leash and runs her hand over his head a few times.

"It's okay," she tells him. "It'll get better."

Still, she wonders how long it'll be before things start to turn a corner for Rugby.

Sheila has to admit Alan was right. Rugby is the most challenging dog she's ever worked with. Despite her best efforts, he's still very emotionally shut down. In more than five years of working as a veterinarian at the Center for Shelter Dogs, she's never seen a dog quite like this one. Typically, the dogs she works with are either extremely fearful or extremely aggressive, and in the case of dogs with fear aggression, both. Rugby is none of these things. Instead, his behavior reminds Sheila of the saying "Still waters run deep." He is still. He is quiet. He is deeply unreachable.

Even so, she's hopeful she'll eventually be able to help him. He's a beautiful dog. He's gentle. If she can get him socialized, get him to connect with people, he'll be a wonderful member of the right family. The way things are going, though, she's coming to understand just how significant the "if" in that thought is. And, odd as the idea may be, Sheila's beginning to wonder if perhaps Rugby's path is different from the one envisioned for him by the people who brought him to safety. A path only he understands; a path interrupted by trapping him at Covanta, and on which she now stands in the way. She has no way of knowing that within days, she'll make a decision that will inadvertently set Rugby back on that path.

By the third week in February, Rugby has been with Sheila for two weeks. She believes he's comfortable enough with his surroundings and her dogs to be given free access to the yard. Pete has the day off. Before heading to work in the morning Sheila asks him to let Rugby out into the yard with their dogs for a bit, see if he might socialize with them. Even just a little.

"And don't forget to unblock the dog door in the shed," she reminds Pete. "He'll probably want to go back inside after a few minutes."

"Yup, got it."

"Okay. Call me later, let me know how it goes." She gathers her keys and purse, puts on her gloves, and heads out the door.

It's afternoon when Pete calls.

"Rugby's gone."

"What do you mean he's gone? Gone where?"

"I was out in the yard with the dogs and Rugby, right by the house, and I could hear the landline ringing. So I went in to answer it. I was only inside for ten minutes, maybe not even. When I went back outside, our dogs were there and Rugby was gone. I don't know where he is."

Sheila struggles to breathe the thick and oddly fuzzy air, feels her insides turn liquid. She's never lost a dog in her care. *Never.* The whole situation is surreal.

"How did he get out? Did someone leave the gate open?" There'd be no reason for anyone to be opening the gate into their yard, but nothing else makes sense. The yard is completely enclosed by a sturdy, six-foot, chain-link fence.

"No. He must've found a section of the fence that was loose. Probably just dug at the ground around it, then pawed or pulled at the fencing until he had an opening. Or maybe he dug the fence loose from the bottom. It must've been a tight squeeze for him either way, but he managed to push his way out."

"Are you serious?"

Never in her wildest imaginings could she have envisioned this scenario. It's difficult to rip even a loose panel of chain-link fencing away from a metal pole, or to dig out from beneath a fence. Extremely difficult. It would be a challenge for her to do it with tools, and it would certainly take her some time. He'd done it with nothing but his paws, and in under ten minutes. *Christ.* No dog she's worked with has ever wanted to escape badly enough to do that. Or been smart enough to figure out how.

"Yeah. Unfortunately, yeah. I'm serious."

"Okay. You need to go out and look for him. Now. I'll call the ARL and tell them he's missing."

It's not a call she's looking forward to making, but they're going to need all the help they can get recovering this dog. Because he's obviously a hell of a lot smarter than anyone's given him credit for.

The days following Rugby's unexpected exit from their yard are difficult for the D'Arpinos. Brian O'Connor at the ARL notifies Beth Corr that Rugby has gone missing, and Beth immediately reaches out to Sheila.

"Get flyers up right away. Not too much detail. Just his picture, the word 'missing,' and the ARL's phone number."

Beth posts Rugby's "Missing" flyer to GSDR's Facebook page. She also e-mails the flyer to every ACO in the towns bordering Stoughton, as well as to those on the South Shore from Quincy to Plymouth. She's sure he'll pop up somewhere; she just has no idea where. And when it comes to recovering a missing dog, she's learned it's always better to over-reach.

Sheila spends the days after Rugby's disappearance incessantly second-guessing herself. Had she misjudged Rugby's readiness for free access to the yard? Had the section of fence he'd escaped through really been separated from the pole? And if so, how long had it gone unnoticed? She also grapples with the fact that, for some people in the shelter community, her losing a dog will call her expertise and professionalism into question. For someone with her reputation as a go-to behaviorist for shelter dogs, this is tough to swallow. But even more painful are her visions of Rugby alone and cold, with no food or shelter, possibly already miles away and headed who knows where.

On March 10, the call they've been waiting for comes. A dog that looks like Rugby has been seen multiple times behind an office building in the neighboring town of Canton. The ARL immediately goes to the location to get a camera and feeding station set up.

Everyone's busy walking around the area, talking back and forth about the best place and angle for the trail camera, and getting the food together. No one notices the black and white dog watching them from his crouched position in the brush just behind the tree line, the commotion fueling his fear. He smells the food they've brought, his stomach reacting to the scent with a growling noise and the pain he's grown so used to. But his instincts tell him to hide. He waits until the humans have left and all is quiet. Then he gulps down the food and runs.

Five

It's been just over two weeks since the last sighting call from Canton. The search for Rugby is ongoing, but stalled. The "Missing" flyer Beth made the day after he escaped from the D'Arpino's yard is still being shared on Facebook, and her best guess is that he's hunkered down somewhere in Canton or Stoughton. But with no sightings to confirm her hunch and, more importantly, pinpoint Rugby's location, setting up cameras or feeding stations is pointless. There are so many other dogs missing in the greater Boston area; dogs whose locations have been confirmed and have trapping procedures underway. Out of necessity, Beth focuses her attention and energy on those dogs, the ones she can actively help.

On March 7, 2012, Underhound Railroad volunteer Mel Katz scrolls through GSDR's Facebook page. A friend's dog is missing, and Mel wants to confirm that the dog's flyer is posted on the page. But it's another posting that grabs her attention, stops her breathing, and halts her scrolling in its tracks. It's a SABER (Safe Animal By Emergency Response) alert from the Animal Control Officers Association of Massachusetts. The alert—the canine equivalent of the Amber Alert system for missing children—is generated by the ACO in Marshfield,

Massachusetts, and featured by GSDR as its "Lost Pet of the Week." And the dog in the photo is a dead ringer for Solomon.

According to the alert, the dog, Rugby, was last seen on February 21, 2012, on Canton Street in Stoughton, Massachusetts. That, Mel thinks, is a long, long way from Kittery. It can't be him. But the dog's posture, facial expression, and unusual bovine-like markings won't allow her to dismiss the possibility that it is. And then there's that large black spot rimming the dog's left eye. Just like the spot around Solomon's left eye.

The description of the dog is on target, too. Pit bull/akita/cattle dog mix, neutered male, 65 pounds, no microchip. Could someone have found or adopted Solomon, named him Rugby, moved from Maine to Massachusetts, and then lost him? It's not impossible, she thinks. But then her rational side takes over. Really, what are the chances of this scenario? It's not him.

Still, she can't fully give in to rationality, can't relinquish her belief that the dog is Solomon. She pulls up Solomon's Facebook page and creates an album called "RUGBY or SOLOMON?" In it, she posts the picture of Rugby from the SABER alert flier, along with a few earlier pictures of Solomon for comparison. The longer Mel looks at the pictures, the more convinced she is that Rugby is Solomon. She writes a comment on the page and tags Hope at Underhound Railroad. Until Hope tells her it's not him, she's not going to stop believing that it is.

When Hope sees the comment from Mel, she feels a distinct shift in the energy around her, the way she often does when something potentially life changing appears out of nowhere.

"Hope, check out this dog. Missing from MA, but he sure looks like (and acts like) Solomon. Look at the black patch patterning on his side. Looks almost like a perfect match, and that's a very unusual pattern. It would be really interesting to contact this person and find out where they got Rugby."

Hope examines the pictures closely, then bursts into tears. It's absolutely him, not one doubt in her mind. The dog she's lost weight, time, sleep, tears, and her car over—the dog her heart has never given up on—is still alive. Of all the miracles in her life, she thinks, this is one of the most wonderful.

She calls the number on the flyer and speaks with Brian O'Connor at the ARL in Boston. He shares the only part of Solomon's story he knows—what happened between Covanta and the most recent sighting in Canton.

"At this point, we're still looking for him."

Hope knows from experience how difficult it is to catch this dog, and how ridiculously smart he is. That he was ever trapped is astonishing.

"How did you trap him?" she asks Brian.

"The folks from GSDR trapped him. We just took him in. You should talk with Beth Corr. She'll be able to tell you the whole story."

Hope calls Beth, heart pounding. She's eager to hear everything Beth knows about Solomon, and to share his past with her. But she's also devastated that he's missing again. He's way too smart to be trapped a second time; she knows this better than anyone. She wonders what the plan is to recover him. Do they even have a plan? It's beginning to feel like December 2010 all over again to her. Only worse, because she already knows what they're in for.

It all comes out in a rush, words tumbling one over another.

"Hi Beth, my name's Hope. You don't know me and I'm calling from Boothbay Harbor in Maine but Rugby the dog that's posted on GSDR's Facebook page is actually an Underhound Railroad rescue dog named Solomon and he went missing in Kittery, Maine in December 2010."

The silence that follows feels like an endless slo-mo someone forgot to dub. But when Beth finally speaks, Hope immediately likes the sound of her voice. Steady and smart. The voice of a person not easily rattled.

"December 2010. From Kittery. Are you sure it's the same dog?"

"A hundred percent sure. I did side-by-side comparisons of the pictures, and it's definitely him. The markings are identical. The pictures are on his Facebook page if you want to see them."

He has his own Facebook page?

"What's it called?"

"Help-us-find-Solomon. With hyphens between the words."

Beth pulls up the page, stares at the photos. She's looked at a lot of side-by-sides over the years, and these are about as absolute as they get. "Yup. Definitely him. Unbelievable. So what's his story?" Beth has the feeling this one's going to be over the top.

"How much time have you got?"

"For this story? Unlimited."

And so Hope starts at the very beginning, in the fall of 2010, and ends with the last confirmed sighting of Solomon in Eliot.

"We kept hoping for another sighting, but we never got another call after that."

"By that time he was probably on his way to Covanta," Beth says.

Hope does the calculations in her head. So this would mean it took him what … six to seven weeks to get from Kittery to Haverhill? That seems not a terribly long time for a dog to travel that far. Especially a dog recovering from heartworm.

"I still can't believe he walked all the way from Kittery to Haverhill. I mean, it's not even a short drive. And he *walked*. In the middle of one of the worst winters ever. With compromised lungs. Honestly, there's a part of me that still can't believe he's alive."

"I know. He's been on quite the journey, that boy."

Beth sits very still on the couch, her brain absorbing the details of her conversation with Hope. It all makes so much sense now. For the first time, she fully understands what they're up against. This is no ordinary dog. His survival skills have been honed to a level she's never encountered. He's the epitome of a survivor, with the ability to outwit them all. If they have any hope of recovering him, they're going to have to raise their game in a major way. It's time to come up with a new plan; something he's never seen before.

She thinks back to Solomon's escape from the D'Arpinos, realizes what a perfect storm had been brewing. The dog is the ultimate flight risk. But no one had known. If Sheila had been aware of his history, Beth is sure she would've made a different decision about allowing him some unleashed time in the yard. She picks up the phone now to call Sheila, who deserves to know everything she didn't know when she'd agreed to work with Solomon/Rugby.

As Sheila listens to Beth's re-cap of Hope's story, the heavy weight of self-blame she's been carrying lifts. The sensation of psychic and physical lightness left behind is delicious. Still, she regrets not having this crucial information from the start. If she had, she probably wouldn't have agreed to work with the dog. And if she *had* chosen to do so, she would've made different decisions, taken things even slower. But her regret morphs into something positive: confidence in Solomon's chances for survival. And his incredible backstory adds another layer of support to something she's been mulling since his escape from her backyard; the possibility that he's looking for something, or someone.

"You know what I think?" she asks Beth.

"What?"

"The only way this dog is going to be able to live with people is if he chooses them himself. Forcing him to interact with people chosen for him is going to continue to be counterproductive. That's my opinion, anyway. For whatever it's worth."

"You may be right," Beth says. Even so, she knows she's not going to stop looking for Solomon. If he's not safely recovered, none of the rest of it matters.

"I hope he finds whatever or whoever he's looking for," Sheila continues. "My wish for him is the same wish I have for every shelter dog. A long, happy life with people who love him."

On that, Beth thinks, they couldn't agree more.

After devouring the food set out for him behind the office building in Canton and running, Solomon's trek takes him in a southeasterly direction. He returns to the pattern of existence that has served him well: he sleeps during the warmer daytime hours and travels, unseen, at night, the continual motion warming his body.

His search for food is constant. Some nights, he finds himself on a street with scraps of food available in upright containers at the end of every driveway. Some of the containers are metal, some are plastic, but all are easily accessible. Other nights there are no containers. There's just an ache in his belly so painful that early sleep or plenty of water are the only remedies.

One night, his search for food and water unsuccessful, he finds himself at one end of a small overpass. As he crosses over it, a loud, whooshing noise rushes beneath him. Then another, and another. He breaks into a run and reaches the other side of the overpass before the next noise shakes the concrete beneath his paws. He then continues onward, heading east.

Solomon has no idea that the noise beneath him is traffic from the hazardous Southeast Expressway. Or that he's found a safe way to cross this six-lane highway by going above rather than across it. But this chance encounter with an overpass will alter his direction of travel and, ultimately, his life.

Six

Solomon weaves his way through a cluster of streets on the eastern side of the Southeast Expressway. In the hours of earliest morning the streets are dark, quiet. He sees not a single human, hears only the occasional dog, alerted to his presence, barking inside a house. Sometimes he stops to listen to those canine communications, though he never barks in response. Other times, he simply moves on.

After searching unsuccessfully for food in one particular neighborhood, Solomon eventually finds his way into an open, grassy area behind it. Just beyond the stretch of dried winter grass are train tracks and he steps onto them without hesitation. He follows the tracks until they fork. Then he stops, stands for a moment. Head tilted slightly backward, nose lifted upward, he inhales every bit of information there is to take in. Then he turns left, following the tracks of the Massachusetts Bay Transit Authority's Greenbush Line.

That first night on the tracks, he walks until he hears the dawn birdsongs. He knows from experience that soon there will be humans moving about, the air will warm, and he will be able to sleep. He looks around for a place to tuck into. Off to his left, parallel to the tracks, he sees an opening in the brush and trees. He veers off the tracks and through the opening, then makes his way up an empty street.

A short distance away he finds a cemetery. Solomon walks around the wrought iron gate and into the cemetery, then heads to the area farthest away from the street, from people. This section of the cemetery abuts the train tracks, perched above them on a knoll. He follows the rows of old, lichened stones until he finds one large enough to fully hide his body. He curls up tightly alongside the cold stone, and, despite the dampness of the ground against his body, falls into a deep, immediate sleep.

But he's soon jolted awake by something moving on the tracks below him. Something large and fast and noisy. His ears ring painfully, and a cold rush of wind rakes his body as the object passes, then disappears. He falls back to sleep, but the object returns again and again, disrupting what uneasy sleep he's able to find in between its appearances.

Fully awake now, the edge of his hunger is sharp. Solomon leaves the cemetery, turns right, then left, and follows the scent of food straight into a busy village. There are cars and people everywhere. He sticks to areas behind buildings, avoiding contact with people. The scent of food surrounds him. Stomach growling and mouth salivating, he moves like a pinball, following his nose in all directions. But though he can smell food everywhere, he can't find it. Exhausted, and even hungrier from the energy he's expended, he returns to the cemetery and waits for darkness.

The team of volunteers working to bring Solomon to safety is worried. The flyers hung on telephone poles and e-mailed to ACOs have "Shy—Do Not Chase!" across the bottom in large, bold black type. Still, there are always people who ignore those words. They're well meaning, wanting to catch the dog and be the hero. But instead of being a hero, the person giving chase almost always makes things worse by setting the dog off into flight mode.

A dog in flight mode is terrified, running blindly across streets and highways, often getting hit, possibly killed. And if the dog manages to avoid that, he usually leaves the area. This ruins any trapping or other recovery plan that was in place and forces volunteers to start all over again with a blank slate, trying to locate the dog in a new area.

The volunteer team hopes Solomon is settled in somewhere safe, that he's established some kind of a routine that will lead to a sighting. They especially hope that whoever spots him also sees his flyer and calls the phone number on it. If the team knew he'd recently been hanging out near the Southeast Expressway, and was now traveling along rail tracks, they wouldn't be sleeping at night.

Dogs surviving on their own are often drawn to rail tracks. The tracks are clear in winter. Travel is more direct, encounters with people minimal. And the linear structure, like that of fences, walls, and cemeteries, appeals to a dog's sense of safety. The dangers of traveling on train tracks, though, can far outweigh the benefits. The team is unaware of any dog who's survived an encounter with a train. Which may be why, at this point, no one is discussing the possibility that he's traveling along active train tracks. Dog recovery people have their superstitions. And one of those superstitions is that you don't talk about things you don't want to happen.

The evening air is chilly and damp when Solomon sets out on the tracks again. Shivering, he steps up his pace. He walks for a little over a mile, and then he hears it. The vibration of steel on cement. He scrambles up a slight incline into the shelter of some leafless brush. The vibrations become a loud rush of air, whipping and whistling through the brambles he crouches beneath. He recognizes the same object he saw from his perch in the cemetery. As it hurtles past him, a shock of cold air combs through his short fur, blows the sensitive tips of his upright ears backward. And then, just as quickly as they arrived, the noise and the wind and the cold are gone.

Solomon remains huddled in the brush until he no longer sees or hears the object, then heads back onto the tracks. He continues picking his way along the cement ties until he comes across another opening alongside the tracks. The platform and parking lot of the Cohasset station are quiet, the last stragglers from the train that passed him already in their cars, headed home.

He follows the tracks almost past the station before he stops abruptly, lifts his nose to the air. Catching the scent of food, he makes his way off the tracks and through the parking lot, nostrils working overtime. He finds what he's looking for in a trash receptacle, the crumpled paper bag near the top an easy grab for him. Standing on his hind legs, Solomon sticks his head into the receptacle and pulls the bag from the pile of trash. His eyes scan for a hiding place. Then, bag in mouth, he walks briskly toward the far end of the parking lot. Concealing himself in the darkness, he rips the bag open and devours its contents.

When the last bit of food has been licked from its wrapper, he heads back through the parking lot toward the tracks. But instead of continuing his travel along the rails as he's done for nearly three weeks, something strong, instinctual, pulls him in the opposite direction. He turns around and walks through the parking lot, then turns right onto East Street. He walks along this street until he comes to an intersection. The street to his left is dark, secluded, and he turns onto it. He continues along this street, traveling northeast, the air's scent growing heavy with salt as he moves closer and closer to the edge of the earth.

If anyone living along Forest Avenue in Cohasset, Massachusetts, had glanced outside at just the right moment on that late-March night in 2012, they might have observed him. An unaccompanied black and white dog with unusual cow-like markings, walking briskly along the empty sidewalk, would've gotten some attention in this leash-law town. But he goes unseen, his presence unreported.

After a mile or so he passes Wheelwright Park. To him, it's nothing more than a large space with grass, trees, and the faint smell of other dogs. At the entrance to this area he stops. He stands, motionless, his senses overloading on information, his body poised for flight at the slightest detection of danger. Once confident in the safety of his surroundings, he ventures off the sidewalk and onto a wooded trail, searching for food and water. Finding nothing in the immediate vicinity, he reverses direction and heads back out to the road.

By now deep darkness has settled, and cars have long since stopped passing along this stretch of road. Solomon travels undisturbed for nearly three more miles, until he comes to a bend in the road. His instincts lead him left, along Atlantic Avenue. Not far up the road, Cohasset becomes Hull. Shortly after passing into Hull he catches a whiff of damp pungency, the scent of things that grow beside water. It's his first source of water in nearly a day. Standing by the edge of Straits Pond he drinks, pauses, then lowers his head again to the water's black, glassy surface. He repeats these actions until his thirst is quenched. Then he continues along Atlantic Avenue, headed north.

At the next major split, Atlantic connects to Nantasket Avenue. Here, Solomon continues traveling northward. The stretch of Nantasket Avenue he's now on is a paradise for a dog surviving on his own. Several restaurants, a couple of hotels, and the Paragon Carousel—the only surviving ride from Paragon Park, Hull's once-famous amusement park— are located feet from each other. Drawn as always by the smell of food, he detours behind the first restaurant he passes to rummage through the trash. The industrial dumpster is closed at the bottom, the trash bags visible on the open top too high for him to reach.

At the neighboring restaurant Solomon's luck improves. A trash bag lies on the pavement, propped up against the overflowing dumpster. The area behind the restaurant is dark and secluded, a safe place to eat. His teeth puncture the bag, his nails then slashing the small puncture into a gaping hole. He devours whatever is edible, the dull and nearly constant ache in his mid-section slowly fading. After rooting through the bag's contents one more time, he walks around the corner of the restaurant and turns back onto Nantasket Avenue. Something continues to guide him northward, insistent, and he continues to follow its pull.

As the first rays of muted light pierce the ocean's horizon, he begins his search for a hiding place. Moving stealthily in and out of yards on the streets between Nantasket Avenue and Beach Street, he looks for a shed. Or a porch with a partially enclosed opening beneath it. Or anywhere else he can tuck into and sleep, unnoticed and undisturbed. Finding nothing suitable in the first few yards, he continues criss-crossing Nantasket and Beach until he notices the perfect spot. It's a salt-weathered front porch, with latticework enclosing the crawl space beneath the floorboards. Not far from where the porch connects to the foundation, a small section of the wooden lattice has rotted away, creating an opening just large enough for him to squeeze through.

Solomon presses through the opening; then, body low, belly grazing the hardened ground, moves into the space until he can go no farther. He lies on the packed dirt beneath the porch, body pressed against the foundation. His eyes peer intently through the lattice, watching for anything that moves in the pink-gray light. But all is still. Exhausted from his night travels, he sleeps.

When Solomon wakes later in the day, the sun is warm and he is thirsty. He flattens himself against the dirt, easing his way out from under the porch with a series of small slithers and twists. He stands, shakes himself, then heads off in search of water. He cuts across a yard, then another, then follows a narrow road straight down to the largest, noisiest body of water he's ever seen.

He watches the water rush forward with a muffled boom, then recede out of reach. Hesitant, he approaches. His tongue laps the water once, but the taste is sharp and bitter. Beneath him, he feels the ground shift. It pulls his paws downward, sucking them into the cold wet sand as even colder water rushes over them and nips at his ankles. He pulls his feet out of the sand and moves away from the water's edge to firmer, drier ground. Unable to drink the water, and unable to travel any farther east, he heads back in the direction of the porch.

He hasn't gotten far when he sees a group of small humans racing toward him, shrieking. Terrified, he turns and runs, heading northward up the beach. He doesn't stop running until there's not a human, large or small, in sight. He slows his pace to a walk, catches his breath. He doesn't return to his shelter under the lattice-enclosed porch. Instead, he keeps walking north along the beach until he finds himself on a peninsula. Unable to walk any farther, Solomon exits the beach. He walks up a slight hill, and soon spots a house every sense tells him is devoid of human activity. Then he curls up in the corner of the house's porch, and doesn't move from this spot until dawn.

When dawn breaks, Solomon uncurls the warm comma of his body. He stretches backward, a long, deep stretch that loosens his muscles after being curled up all night. He gives himself an enthusiastic body shake, then trots down the steps of the porch in search of food. Down the hill near the beach, there's a marshy area. From previous experience he knows there are small animals living in the tall grass. He pushes his way into and through the reeds, following his nose until he's rewarded with some rodents.

As the sky becomes lighter, he exits the marsh and crosses the street, then travels briefly along the sidewalk. But at the sound of fast-moving human steps and loud, measured breathing behind him, he races off the sidewalk into a deserted yard. Dashing up the empty driveway until he's out of sight, he hears the human run by. When he's sure the human is gone, Solomon takes a walk around the backyard of the house. Like the house where he spent the previous night, he can tell by the silence and lack of human scents that this house, too, is empty. As he pokes around the property, sniffing, he finds a small shed. The window is broken, but low to the ground. Solomon walks over to the window, sniffs deeply. Satisfied by the information his sense of smell relays, he bends his hind legs slightly, then jumps through the window into the shed.

Seven

The first call to Hull ACO Leslie Badger comes sometime during the late morning of April 1, 2012. The caller is a woman at a familiar address on Newton Street in Hull Village, the swankiest part of town: lovely Victorians, sprawling yards, and killer views of the Atlantic Ocean on one side and Quincy Bay on the other.

"I'm calling because there's a dog in my backyard, sunning himself. He's wearing a collar; I'm pretty sure it's my neighbor's pit bull again. He's not causing trouble or anything, but I know he's not supposed to be loose."

"Okay, no problem. I'll be right over."

Gathering up her keys and phone and heading out the door, Leslie doesn't bother to grab her rabies pole. She's been called to pick up this particular dog from the woman's yard, as well as other neighbors' yards, on several occasions, knows he's friendly. She has no reason to expect she'll need to do anything more complicated than walk up to him, hook a leash onto his collar, put him in the ACO van, and drive him home. Again. And this time, she intends to give his owners not only another reminder that the town has a leash law, but a formal warning about their continuing non-compliance.

Despite the bright sunshine, the air carries the chill that passes for early spring in New England. The van's cold steering wheel against her bare hands makes Leslie briefly consider going back inside for her gloves, but it doesn't seem worth the extra time. The van's heat will kick in soon enough. She backs out of the driveway and drives northeast to Hull Village.

When Leslie arrives at the yard on Newton Street the dog is stretched out on his side in the sun, just as the caller described. She gets out of the van, leash in hand, and walks toward him. He suddenly raises his head off the ground and looks at her. Leslie's reflexive inhalation of air through her mouth is sharp, audible. And then time stands still.

This isn't the pit bull she's expecting to see. It's Solomon, whose disappearance from Stoughton had set off a frantic search, his "missing dog" flyer sent to every ACO on the South Shore. His whereabouts have remained a mystery ... until now. It's him. She's stared at that flyer so many times, enough to have committed the dog's striking face, his unusual markings, to memory. It's definitely him.

Leslie regrets having left her rabies pole at home and considers going back for it. The likelihood of recovering this particular dog using only a leash is laughably low. Still, she's sure that even if her movement back across the yard to the van doesn't spook him, seeing her re-approach with a rabies pole will. She decides to stay put, try to approach him slowly. If he'll let her.

It's a dicey decision. The layout of the yard isn't set up in her favor. One side of the property is fenced, the other side wide open. She studies its configuration, trying to determine the angle of approach most likely to keep him in the yard.

Inching closer and closer to him, she doesn't speak, averts her eyes to avoid direct contact with his. He continues to watch her, head lifted. Then he springs up and over the fence. Up and over so fast, she barely registers the individual components of the action.

He's gone.

The woman who called Leslie to report the dog in her yard comes outside to chat.

"Once I saw him get up, I could tell he was too big to be my neighbor's dog. I don't know whose dog he is. I've never seen him around here before. There's something about him, though. Something kind of … I don't know. Intriguing, I guess, is the best word for it."

Leslie stares for a long moment at the fence Solomon has just vanished over, then turns to the woman.

"Oh, he's intriguing, alright. You have no idea."

Back in the van, Leslie sets off to look for Solomon, who has seemingly evaporated into thin air. After multiple loops through Hull Village, she pulls over to the side of the road and calls the number listed on Solomon's "missing dog" flyer.

Beth Corr is walking her dogs in a Brookline park when her cell phone rings.

"Hey, this is Leslie Badger, the ACO in Hull. You're never going to believe who I just saw."

Leslie is smiling; Beth can hear it in her voice. Excellent. Whatever news the Hull ACO is calling to share is likely good. Beth mentally flips through the "missing dog" flyers from the Boston area. Is there a dog missing that far down on the South Shore? She can't think of one at the moment, but why else would the Hull ACO be calling her? She gives up.

"Who?"

"Solomon! He's in Hull."

Beth is stunned.

"*What?* No…He can't be!" Hull is, quite literally, the end of the earth, a peninsula surrounded by the ocean to the east and bays to the north and west. What would he be doing there? Of all the places she'd considered most likely for Solomon to pop up in, Hull wasn't even a contender. It has to be a mistake. Probably some black and white dog resembling him.

"He is! I just saw him in someone's yard in Hull Village. When I tried to get close, he jumped over the chain link fence and took off. I swear to God, it was him."

As the conversation continues, Solomon suddenly reappears. He stands on the sidewalk and looks both ways, waiting for a clear opening in the traffic. Then he crosses the street, almost directly in front of the ACO van.

"Oh my God, he's right in front of me!"

"Get a picture if you can."

Leslie snaps some quick shots of a beautiful, graceful dog in motion, trotting briskly across the street. His posture and attitude convey a sense of purpose, of confidence. She has no idea where he's headed, but he clearly knows exactly where he's going. This isn't just idle wandering, she thinks. He's on a mission. She texts the photos to Beth, then waits for a response.

In the park in Brookline, Beth stares at the images. It's him, no doubt about it. When she gets home, she'll do a side-by-side comparison of the photos she already has of him with the ones Leslie just took. But really, that will be just a formality. The dog in the photos Leslie took is absolutely Solomon. Somehow, for some reason, he has indeed managed to travel from Stoughton to Hull.

Beth does a quick search for "distance between Stoughton MA and Hull MA." According to Google, the actual distance between the towns is 15.8 miles and some change, the driving distance 25.6 miles. It's a long way for a dog to travel in a little under three weeks. And then there's the Southeast Expressway. Heavily traveled, even at night, the Expressway stretches from Braintree to Sagamore, separating the western South Shore towns from those along the coast.

Solomon went missing in Stoughton on February 21, and the last confirmed sighting call came in on March 10 from Canton, just to the southwest. To get to Hull from Canton, located off Route 24, he would've first had to get himself to the Expressway. Then he would have had to cross three lanes in both directions and, depending on his location, negotiate a bank of Jersey barriers separating the northbound and southbound lanes. The plentiful roadkill she's seen along the edges of the highway is testament to the challenge of getting from one side to the other.

But given her previous experience with this dog, Beth believes almost anything is possible. He could have swum across Quincy Bay to Hull on a dead-low tide. He might've even been able to walk most of the way if the water was low enough. Coyotes have walked across the bay on an ebb tide and taken up residence on a few of the Harbor Islands. There's no reason why Solomon couldn't also have crossed the bay on foot. Or maybe he jumped into the flatbed of a parked truck, fell asleep, and was transported to Hull by an unsuspecting driver. He could have traveled on a surface road, and gone under the highway, or maybe come across one of the few overpasses. And what about railroad tracks? Her mind spins at the possibilities. It's too much for her brain to process all at once. She closes the text and calls Leslie.

"Yup. It's him. If I hadn't seen the pictures, I wouldn't have believed it. But it's definitely him. Incredible."

They talk for a while longer, making plans for Beth to drive down to Hull Village, meet with Leslie, and figure out a strategy to recover Solomon. That settled, Beth loads her dogs into the car and heads home. She has many phone calls to make regarding this latest chapter in Solomon's story. The D'Arpinos are right up there at the top of her list, but her first call will be to Hope at Underhound Railroad.

Leslie and Beth are in the ACO van, touring Hull Village.

"So the first call came from a woman in this house right here," Leslie says, pointing out the yard on Newton Street where she'd seen Solomon basking in the sun a little over a week ago.

Beth scans the area surrounding the house.

"Interesting. Did the caller happen to see the direction he came from?"

"Unfortunately, no."

Having this bit of specific information might help them find

Solomon's home base. Every missing dog has a home base. Knowing its location can help streamline the process of choosing the best place to set a camera, food, water, and, if needed, a trap. Beth is confident they'll eventually figure out exactly where he's bedding down. But for now, having even a general vicinity to focus on is good enough for her.

Leslie drives to the end of Newton Street and stops in front of the house directly across from them, at the intersection of Newton and Highland Street. The house, an enormous Victorian with a large yard, carries an air of desertion. Next door, at the bottom of the hill where Highland intersects with Main Street, is the Coast Guard station.

"This is another house he's been seen at," Leslie says. "Nobody's living here right now; might be a summer home. But I've gotten a few calls from neighbors, saying they've seen him use this yard and the Coast Guard property as a cut-through. I called the Coast Guard station, and they've seen him, too."

"Where does he go from there?"

"To the beach. The marshes. He probably hunts in the marshes."

"Could be. Hope has video footage that a guy up in Eliot, Maine, shot of Solomon killing ducks along the river when he was still in that area."

"Whatever he's hunting here, he must be eating it right there in the marshes where no one can see him. Because I haven't gotten a single call about him killing anything."

Leslie takes a left on Highland, driving up the hill and around a slight curve. She pulls over to the side of the road in front of another house, its side lawn a long gentle slope to the bay.

"He's been seen here a few times, too. This one's another summer property, so it's empty right now. And quiet. There's a porch he can lie on out back, up high and hidden from the street."

"Can we get out and look around?" Beth asks.

"Sure."

The scent of intermingled sunlight and salt wafts up from the bay as Beth and Leslie make their way down the yard to the water. Beth smiles, inhales deeply. From the water's edge she can see across the bay to Quincy and Weymouth, and she wonders again how Solomon got to Hull. Could he really have walked and swum his way across the bay on an ebb tide? She wishes she knew, but unless someone steps up and says they saw him crossing the bay, it's likely they'll never have the answer to that question. She turns away from the water and heads back to the van.

Halfway up the sloping yard Beth stops to catch her breath, taking the opportunity to give the backyard a closer look. To her left, she notices a small area set back a bit from the house. It's completely shielded from the street, sheltered from the wind off the bay by a few bushes, and very flat. She walks over to Leslie.

"That area right there could be a good place to set up a camera and a trap," she says, pointing. "Very quiet, very private."

"I was thinking the same thing."

They trudge the rest of the way up the incline together. Back in the van Leslie makes a U-turn, then drives down Highland to the Coast Guard station and takes a right onto Main.

"Another place he's been seen at is Fort Revere Park," she tells Beth, turning left onto Nantasket Avenue. A quick right brings them onto Farina Road, a loop street with the historic look-out site park perched at the very top.

"Definitely want to get out and have a look around here," Beth says.

They park the van and head in the direction of the buildings.

As they walk toward the stone structures, Beth takes mental notes. A couple of picnic tables. A few trash barrels set back twenty feet or so from the tables. She walks over to the trash barrels, pushes them gently. They're unsecured, made of plastic, and tip without much effort. They're also not that high. Easy pickings for a tall, determined dog. She's not sure how consistently reliable a food source these trash receptacles are. But they're likely one of the things that have drawn him to the place.

Beth and Leslie continue on toward the crest of the hill, stopping to look inside one of the buildings. There's no door; just a simple opening cut into the stone, making it easy for a dog to enter and take shelter inside. Still, Beth doubts this is a hiding place. Too public in the daytime, too open at night, ground littered with broken glass. No dog would consider this space a refuge.

When they arrive at the top of the hill, Beth notices something interesting. The buildings' roofs are easily accessible and covered with grass, like the roofs of Irish sod houses. Dogs on their own seek out high places like these. The far-ranging view of approaching predators—and approaching people—makes them feel more secure. Beth wonders if, on a quiet, sunny day, Solomon might hide himself in the tall rooftop grass for a sunbath or even a nap.

"I can see why he's attracted to this place," she says. "When people called about seeing him up here, did they say what he was doing?"

"Rummaging around the trash cans, mostly."

"So it sounds like it's mainly about food." Maybe the trash receptacles are reliable after all, Beth thinks. Too bad the place is a state park with human activity and liability issues. Otherwise, it would be a good location to set up a camera and feeding station. Still, it helps to know about this area in terms of understanding his behavior, establishing his patterns.

They drive around some more, eventually parking by the water facing Hingham Bay.

"I'd give a million dollars to anyone who could tell me how Solomon got to Hull," Beth says, staring out across the water.

"I know. It's just crazy. I mean, why here?"

"I don't know. Sometimes, dogs on the run do keep heading toward the ocean. Just keep going, 'til they can't go any farther. But he went missing from Stoughton … so why didn't he head to Quincy, to Quincy Bay? Much closer, and a straighter shot."

"Exactly."

They're silent for a moment, gazing at the bay, contemplating the question. Beth turns to Leslie.

"How do you think he got here? Do you think he swam?"

"Well, I guess he could've walked, right? But if he did, I don't think he walked along the highway. I think he picked up the rail tracks somewhere and followed them here. He could've gotten off the tracks at Cohasset, or at Nantasket Junction, and then walked from either right into Hull."

"That's one possibility. Pretty common for dogs to travel the tracks," Beth says.

"Could he have swum here? I don't know; the water in the bay's really choppy. But on a super low tide, the water almost disappears between World's End over in Hingham and the shoreline right by the Hull library. Which is very close to the area of Hull Village where the first sighting call came from. And the water in that area of the bay's much calmer. So yeah, I guess if he caught the tide just right, he could've swum from World's End."

"You know, when we finally recover this boy my only regret will be that he can't talk."

"I know exactly what you mean. So you really think we'll be able to recover him?"

"Absolutely. But it's going to be a challenge. I've never seen a dog this smart. We *will* prevail, though. Because if there's one thing I hate, it's being outsmarted by a dog."

Leslie laughs. The conversation moves to possible options for recovery; most likely a trap, but potentially a drop-net.

"Have you ever used a net?" Beth asks.

"No. We don't even have one." A drop-net—a trapping method consisting of a net supported by poles and triggered remotely to drop on the dog, tangling him up in the netting—is beyond the town's budget.

"Same here. If we end up going with a drop-net, we'll have to use the ARL's. And we'll definitely need their help; it's tricky to set up and operate. I'm hoping we'll be able to trap Solomon, since getting the net set up is such a complicated, time-consuming process. And then it needs to be monitored carefully once it's set. So probably not our go-to method. But, still an option."

Leslie pushes an errant section of long hair behind her ear. "It'd be great if we could trap him, for sure. But I really wonder if he'll go anywhere near a trap. Especially if we use the same trap he was caught in at Covanta."

"I agree. Very possible he won't go in it. I think it's even less likely he'll go in a standard trap, though. It probably makes the most sense to start with the Gypsy trap."

Thinking about the Gypsy trap brings Beth back to the earliest recovery attempts at Covanta. The moment she'd first seen his picture on the trail camera, the moment she'd known she'd play a significant role in recovering him. She just never imagined the twists and turns it would all take. Or that they'd still be at it, months after they'd thought it was finished.

On the way back to Beth's parked car, they make plans for her to return to Hull Village in the next few days with a couple of GSDR folks. They'll drive around as a group, scout out the locations Beth and Leslie saw today, then make a joint decision on the best place to set a feeding station and trail camera. In the meantime, maybe Leslie will get a few more sighting calls, a few more hints as to exactly where Solomon's home base might be.

After Beth leaves, Leslie drives around Hull Village for a while, hoping to catch sight of Solomon. Nothing. She then heads to the Nantasket Junction train station. Standing on the platform, she studies the open tracks. There's enough room, at least on the section of tracks within her range of vision, for a dog walking them to get out of the way of a train. Plenty of scrubby brush alongside to hide in. He could've definitely come this way, eventually ending up by the restaurants and clubs on Nantasket Avenue. To her, this route makes more sense than his heading in the opposite direction, toward the pristine woods and trails of World's End.

Getting back into the van, she drives a bit farther and pulls into the Cohasset station parking lot. A smaller, quieter station than Nantasket Junction, he could also have gotten off the tracks here. If he did, he would've found darker, less-traveled streets and a small body of water, and would've ultimately ended up at the same strip along Nantasket Avenue with the clubs and the restaurants and the tantalizing aromas of food.

She can't prove it. As far as she knows, no one saw Solomon entering Hull. Still, there's something about the Cohasset station that feels rights to her. For whatever it's worth, her opinion is that this is where he began his trek into Hull.

What she doesn't know, not yet, is why. Why would Solomon travel all the way to Hull, when he could have gotten off the tracks at so many other places along the way? What had drawn him here? Leslie senses that figuring out the answers to these questions is going to be the most rewarding challenge of her career. And, quite possibly, the most transformative. She's grateful to be working with Beth and her team to recover Solomon. It's going to take their combined brain power, and probably some luck, to outsmart him. And she's not entirely convinced even those will be enough. With this dog, they might also need a touch of divine intervention.

PART TWO

Hull
Village

Eight

Lisa Parsons stands on the porch of her yellow Victorian home, gloved hands cupped around a mug of tea. The early night breeze off the water, though chilly, carries that first heady, earthy scent of spring. It always seems so ephemeral to her, this time of year. A season between seasons, precious in all its promise, then gone without a trace. She leans her full weight against a pillar, grateful for the substance and support of it. They really knew how to build things back then, she thinks. Things that were meant to last—the complete opposite of the trail of steam rising from her tea and evaporating into darkness, a visual metaphor for the current state of her life.

She sets the mug on the railing, buttons her thickly knit hoodie sweater all the way up, and slips the hood over her head. Much better. She picks up the mug, takes a sip of tea. Sleepy-Time. She needs it. Though it's a clear night, she detects a sudden change in the scent of the air, the smell of impending rain. Good, she thinks. It's time for the world to wake up again, to turn green, to blossom. Time for everything to flourish.

It's been a long and emotionally challenging year, and she's not even four months into it. As she and her husband Dave continue to grow further apart, the many ways in which they're ill-suited for each other become increasingly evident. She reaches back into the past, re-winding the years. How long has it been since their marriage was good? Far too long to remember. She loves Dave, and always will. But it's a platonic, love-you-like-a-brother kind of love, not the you're-the-absolute-love-of-my-life kind of love she craves. They probably never should've gotten married. But if they hadn't, there'd be no Ella. And *that*, life without her daughter, she cannot begin to fathom.

But the early months of this year have been the loneliest of her life. The kind of loneliness that happens when you choose to stay in a marriage that's beyond the point of resurrection, and the price of that choice is being required to pretend everything's fine. She doubts, now, the wisdom of her decision to stay. But she can't seem to find a way to leave. Out on the porch under the early April half-moon, she looks up at its light, throws her arms outward, and prays for the unconditional love and faithfulness she needs.

She stands on the porch a while longer, arms wrapped around her body against the chill. She takes three deep breaths, the word "gratitude" the mantra for each inhale and exhale, then picks up her empty mug and goes inside.

Solomon wakes with an urgent sensation of pressure in his bladder and a rumbling pain in his stomach. He rises from the floor of the shed and stretches his body backward, deep and low, his chest grazing the splintered floor. After an abbreviated forward stretch he shakes his body, the motion traveling from his head to the tip of his tail. Then he hops out the window, avoiding the jagged glass jutting from the frame. Once outside he trots briskly down the driveway with its still-hard dirt, small chunks of broken-down asphalt, and overgrown grass. He crosses the street, headed toward the marsh to relieve his bladder and hunt for something to ease the emptiness in his belly. But he doesn't stay long. Finding nothing moving around in the marsh, nothing to pounce on and eat, he pushes his way out of the dry, wheat-colored grass. He stands on the sidewalk, looks both ways. Then he crosses the street and heads west up the hill in the direction of his favorite sunbathing spot, the secluded back deck of a vacant summer home.

By now, most aspects of Solomon's surroundings are familiar to him. The view from the hill at the fort. The multiple routes from one hangout to the next, and the shortest way to get to and from each. Which areas of the marsh provide the best opportunities for food, which dumpsters are accessible. When he's cold, he knows the best places to lie peacefully in the sun, unseen. And his finely calibrated internal clock alerts him to when the dumpster at Jo's Nautical Bar up the street on the bayfront will provide him with an easy meal.

But on this day, he finds an even easier meal. He smells it before he sees it, a small, furry body lying in the road right up against a lawn. Solomon lifts the still-warm animal off the asphalt and trots off with it, heading toward his shed. He stops for a moment, gently drops his find onto the grass. Then he picks it up again, re-adjusts the distribution of the animal's weight in his mouth, and moves on.

A few weeks after first seeing Solomon, Leslie Badger answers a call from a frantic Hull Village resident.

"Oh my God, there's a wild pit bull in my yard, eating the remains of some animal! You have to come get him—there are cats in this neighborhood, and children…"

The woman speaks so fast Leslie can barely follow the story.

"So the dog is actually in your yard?"

"Yes, on the edge. Right near the street."

"And it's still there?"

"*Yes!*"

"Okay, I'll be right over."

A large, possibly feral dog eating an animal. This could get ugly. She glances into the back of the van to make sure her rabies pole is there, then drives off toward the all-too-familiar address: Newton Street. When she arrives at the caller's home, the tiny hairs on the back of her neck tingle and rise. The house is next door to the house where she'd first seen Solomon sunbathing in the yard. Could the dog this woman saw be Solomon?

Leslie knocks on the door. The woman who opens it extends her hand, introduces herself as Lisa Parsons. Still quite upset, Lisa tells Leslie the dog is no longer in her yard.

"I think he may not have actually been eating the animal when I saw him, just putting it down for a minute. Because then I saw him pick it up and walk off. Still, I do think he may be feral. Something about the way he looked around before he picked the animal up says feral to me."

"Can you describe the dog? And do you know for sure it's a male?"

"Big, so I assume male. Not fat, but tall. Black and white. Unusual looking, with markings kind of like a cow. And I'm sure this sounds completely crazy, but the first thing that went through my mind when I saw him was that he's from another century. There's something so old about him. He looks dusty, in the way something very old does. And his collar's leathery and crusty, kind of ancient looking. I just got the sense that he's not of the present, this sense of the otherworldly." She stops, shakes her head self-consciously. "Sorry…I don't know how to describe it."

She doesn't need to. Leslie understands exactly what Lisa is trying to explain, has seen and experienced it for herself. The dog Lisa saw in her yard is Solomon. Leslie's sure of it. She hopes Lisa will be able to answer, in the affirmative, the question she's about to ask.

"When he left your yard, did you see where he went?"

"Yes. I watched him walk to the back of the yard, over by my daughter Ella's playhouse. He kept going in that direction, so I think he probably went down the path that leads to the house behind mine; that abandoned house that's falling apart. Maybe he cut through an opening in the fence after that, because I didn't see him again."

Finally.

Leslie and Beth have spent hours discussing where Solomon's home base might be, how important finding it is to ultimately recovering him. But the "village" part of Hull Village is a misnomer. This section of town isn't tiny, and they have no idea where he might be sleeping. His options are endless. Which is great for him, but not so much for them. Now they potentially have something concrete to work with.

Leslie knows a dog carrying food in his mouth is headed to a place of safety, a place where he can eat unobserved. For Solomon this could mean the marshes. Still, she thinks he's more likely to choose someplace closer, someplace he considers "home." It's like watching the pieces of a puzzle fall into place, all at once. Everything makes sense now. A rickety abandoned house, its proximity to the fort and the bay and the marshes, the way it backs up to Newton Street. It all makes perfect sense.

"Well the good news is, I'm almost a hundred percent sure the dog you saw isn't a wild pit bull. He's a dog a lot of people have been looking for over the last year and a half. His name's Solomon."

As Leslie shares the details of Solomon's long, circuitous journey from Georgia to Kittery to Hull Village, she pulls out her phone and shows Lisa the pictures of Solomon she's taken, along with the ones Beth shared. Lisa looks closely at the photos. "Yes, that's definitely the same dog," she says.

And then a memory of a forgotten incident comes rushing back to her … a sensory recall of swerving car and screeching tires and burning rubber, of a large black and white dog racing across the street in front of her one morning back in March. A black and white dog she'd barely avoided hitting. She now knows that dog was Solomon.

Lisa believes that whatever happens in life is part of a greater plan. She didn't hit Solomon that morning because he wasn't meant to die. And beyond her and her car, there'd been so many other opportunities for him to not make it. Yet he'd cheated death each time, surviving every danger Leslie had described to her: heartworm, freezing cold winters, lack of food and water, travel on roads and highways and tracks, through woods where there had to have been packs of coyotes, and who knew what else. Solomon has survived, she believes, because there's a specific purpose to his life, to his incredible journey. She hopes he finds whatever that purpose is in Hull Village. He's been traveling long enough.

"The bad news is," Leslie continues, "we haven't been able to trap him, or figure out where his home base is. Do you have a few minutes to walk me down through your yard and show me where he went?"

"Of course. I'm happy to help in any way I can."

Leading Leslie down the porch steps and into the yard, Lisa's heart aches for Solomon. Dogs are pack animals, she knows, and she imagines how lonely he must be. He belongs with a family who loves him, not out on his own killing his food or scavenging in dumpsters or picking up roadkill. That's no life for a dog.

"That's where I first saw him, right up there," she says, pointing toward a spot in her yard very close to the street. "He stopped and sat down for a minute, which is when I freaked out and called you. Then he got up and picked up whatever it was he had and walked down here."

As Lisa narrates, they walk past Ella's pink playhouse, then past a couple of pine trees and some tall rhododendron bushes. And there, just as Lisa described, is a path leading to a tall chain-link fence. On the other side is the completely overgrown yard of an abandoned house. Definitely inhospitable for people, Leslie thinks. Which is what makes it perfectly hospitable for Solomon.

Leslie follows the path to the fence for a closer look. The fence is anchored into a cement retaining wall that has what she estimates to be a four-foot-plus drop into the yard. This is a fairly good-sized drop, even for a large dog like Solomon. Still, it looks like any leap down into the yard would be cushioned by layers of dried-up leaves, the apparent accumulated detritus of many autumns. When was the last time anyone lived here? She can't believe the town hasn't condemned this place.

She begins inspecting the fence for loose sections, or gaps beneath the chain-link large enough for Solomon to squeeze under. As she looks to the far left of the fence, she sees that the last panel is placed at a right angle, providing a property boundary marker but no further fencing. Interesting. So he doesn't even have to jump onto or off of the wall, she thinks. He can just walk right around that last panel, then up the slope into Lisa's yard or down the slope into this abandoned yard. Easy.

Scanning the backyard, Leslie notices a white shed off to the side of the house, just a bit behind it. Like the house, the shed is in a state of complete disrepair. Its paint is peeling, one of the window panes broken. If Solomon's home base is somewhere on this property, it's not the safest place he could've chosen. There are pieces of plywood with jagged edges scattered about, and those are just the visible hazards. She's sure there are invisible hazards as well; nails from the plywood, broken glass from the window, and a shed that's probably full of junk and rusty tools. She's keen to take a closer look around. But when she does, she'll drive over and park in the driveway instead of walking down a slope into a covering of leaves with who knows what hiding beneath it.

"I think there's an excellent chance his home base is somewhere down there," Leslie says.

Lisa stands beside her, surveying the house and out-buildings.

"Do you think it's under the front porch, maybe? Or do you think it's in the shed?"

"Could be either. Given the condition of this place, there are probably plenty of areas around the porch where he could squeak through and get underneath it. I'll have to search around the property to know for sure. But my gut tells me his home base is in the shed. It's at the back of the property, away from Main Street traffic. It's much quieter."

"That makes sense. So what's the next step?"

"I'll check the place out tomorrow morning. If this *is* his home base, I'm pretty sure he's down there right now, with whatever he was carrying. The worst thing I could do is flush him out. He feels safe there. I don't want to spook him from a place he's settled into and be back to square one."

"If you need my yard for anything, or if I can help in any other way, please let me know."

"Thanks, Lisa. For now, I think the most helpful thing would be to keep an eye out for him. If you see him, make a note of what direction he's heading in and call me."

These are all things Lisa can do, looks forward to doing. The dog's story, the loneliness she imagines him experiencing, has struck a deep chord within her. There'll be no peace for her soul, she knows, until Solomon is finally wherever it is he's meant to be.

Leslie's van pulls into the driveway of the house on Main Street. The house is heavy with that eerie vibe abandoned buildings give off; a kind of deep, resigned sadness that the life they once harbored has, for whatever reason, moved on. She wonders what happened here. For a brief moment she feels sorry for the house, the lack of attention from its former residents scrawled across its every peeling, rotting clapboard. The desolation of it is starting to get to her.

"Shake it off," she admonishes herself. "It's just a house."

She gets out of the van and approaches the front porch. This morning she's wearing jeans, heavy leather gloves, and a pair of thick-soled boots; a tetanus shot is not on her agenda for the day. A thick pile of dried leaves nearly obscures the steps leading up to the door. Thank God she doesn't have to climb them to ring the bell and notify the owners that she'll be poking around their property for a while. If she did, her foot would probably go right through the rotting wood she suspects is under all those leaves. And the porch roof … holy crap. With layers of leaves and a couple of branches blown off nearby trees weighing on it, a complete collapse seems a distinct possibility.

All in all, the front of the house looks just as dilapidated as the rear. Pretty much what she'd expected. She walks the outside circumference of the porch, looking for breaks in the wooden latticework that encloses the space beneath the floorboards. A visual measure of the height of that space looks to be about three and a half to four feet. That's plenty high for Solomon to comfortably stand up and move around in. It's a large space, too, spanning the width of the house plus a depth she estimates to be fifteen feet. In fact, it may be too large. Dogs generally prefer smaller, tighter spaces. Still, it would be irresponsible of her not to check this area.

Leslie expects to find multiple areas where the lattice has rotted away, but to her surprise this isn't the case. The once-white paint has been neglected into a blistered, peeling shade of light gray, but the wood isn't rotted anywhere. There's no way for a dog to get in under the porch. Well, scratch that one off the list, she thinks. One space down, one to go.

Actually, make that two. She's just about to head over into the back-yard when she notices a space beneath the front steps. Partially hidden on one side by a forked tree and overgrown vegetation, it provides a small, sheltered location between the steps and the lattice. The space is pitched at the same angle as the steps. At its highest point, it's the same height as the crawl space under the porch. He could definitely tuck in there. Dead leaves have blown their way beneath the steps, piling up into what would be a soft, well-insulated nest. Probably a little too exposed for night-time sleeping, she thinks. But for ducking out of sight, or even for a short day-time nap? Perfect. Leslie adds this location to her mental list of Solomon's potential hiding places.

Making her way back up the driveway toward the rear of the house, she sees Lisa's beautiful Victorian on the knoll above her. Flashes of its cheerful yellow peek through the soon-to-be-leafed-out trees. Every once in a while, Leslie just *knows* something. It could be anything. But what-ever it is, she knows it with absolute certainty. And right now, looking at Lisa's house through the trees, she knows that this decrepit property is indeed Solomon's home base. He sleeps here, carries animals he kills or picks up from the street here. Setting off in any direction from this tan-gled, overgrown mess of a backyard easily brings him to the places where he's been seen. This is it. Everything he needs is right here. Including Lisa's house, which for some reason she feels a strange pull toward. She doesn't know what that's about, but wonders if Solomon feels it, too.

As she gets closer to the outbuildings, she notices that the small shed isn't free-standing. It's attached to a building that looks like it might have been either a small summer house for guests or a children's playhouse. This structure is larger than the shed, with an odd set-up. At its front, instead of the usual single door in the middle, are two doors on either side of center. Or, more precisely, an opening where a door once was on the left side, and an actual door on the right side. Between the doors is a two-over-two window. Could he be in there? And what will she do if he is?

Approaching the building quietly is impossible; every step shuffles and crunches the brown leaves beneath her feet. So much for stealth tactics. But then she realizes that if he was anywhere on the property when she first pulled into the driveway, he's long gone by now. Her silence at this point doesn't matter. Not even a little bit.

She peeks in through the window, its glass streaked with years of dust and salt and pollen. Still, it's clear enough for her to see the uncluttered space inside. Just a few miscellaneous yard things leaning up against the far wall. This is too open, she thinks. Too big. He wouldn't hide in there, especially with that one open door. No, he's much more likely to be hanging out in the shed. She walks over to inspect the smaller structure.

Within a few feet of it, the skin on her arms prickles with goose-bumps. From a dog's perspective, this is the most perfect hiding place she's ever seen. From her own perspective, though, the place is one massive injury waiting to happen. The white wooden door is cracked open, though not wide enough for Solomon to pass through. She tugs hard at the door, but it won't budge. In front of the opening is a warped, jagged piece of old plywood, large enough to cover the lower third of the door. This definitely isn't an entrance point, which means he's going in through the only other opening—the window with half its pane broken out. Most of the broken glass rests in an intact sheet on the floor off to the side of the window frame. The remainder sits on top of the folded aluminum frame of a beach chair. She gives her eyes a chance to adjust to the darker areas farthest from the window. After determining the safest path of entry, she climbs through the window frame.

Inside, junk extends in all directions. A collection of rusted hoes and an equally rusted saw. Underneath them, the corner of what looks like an old mover's blanket. An odd, unfamiliar tool resembling a pair of garden shears a giant might use. A moth-eaten gray blanket covered with what looks to her to be black and white dog fur; planks of wood; an overturned white plastic bucket; and a bunch of other metal things she can't identify. It certainly doesn't look like the most comfortable place, but he could lie on that tattered gray blanket and at least get himself off the floor. Other than that, the place is entirely inhospitable. It's the perfect place for this particular dog to hide.

The next day, Leslie, Beth, Lisa, and Ella gather around a trap in Lisa's yard. It's set up a short distance from Ella's playhouse, in a grove of trees near the cut-through to the yard below on Main Street. The trap isn't the Gypsy trap used at Covanta. The grove feels too small and tight for the Gypsy trap. Instead, Leslie and Beth decide to go with a standard large wildlife trap, the kind they'd normally use for recovering a dog of Solomon's size. Beth adjusts the height of the trip plate.

"Does that look about right?" she asks Leslie.

"I think so." Leslie lifts the back panel and reaches into the trap, putting the amount of pressure she believes Solomon's weight would exert onto the trip plate. The front panel of the trap drops smoothly into place. Perfect. She'd picked up a fresh rotisserie chicken on her way over to Lisa's, and she and Beth pull large strips of still-hot meat off the bones, releasing the aroma into the air. They hope Solomon is somewhere close enough to catch the scent.

The trip plate readjusted and the chicken piled onto a disposable plastic plate, Beth demonstrates the workings of the trap to Lisa. Because the trap is in her yard, Lisa will reset it and replenish the food every day. Beth is grateful. In her experience, things always go more smoothly when a home owner who's given permission to set the trap on their property is responsible and eager to become involved.

"Okay, Lisa, the trip plate's already set to the right height. You don't have to touch that at all," Beth says.

"Okay."

"All you have to do is reach in and pull out the plate, then replace it with a new plate of food. You may need to reset the front door panel afterwards."

"How far in should the food go?" Lisa asks.

"Beyond the trip plate. Otherwise, he might be able to grab the edge of the plate and pull it backward out of the trap without stepping on the trip plate."

"Got it. And the front panel?"

"Ah! The tricky part. So with that, it's kind of a balancing act. This skinny bar here, that pulls up? The edge of the panel has to be balanced on the bar's little curved area. If it's not, the panel will fall. Go ahead and play around with it. Once you get the feel for where the right balance point is, it's pretty easy to set."

Lisa pulls the front panel up and outward, balancing the inside edge on the curve of the bar as instructed. The panel holds for a few seconds, then comes crashing down, closing the trap.

"That's okay. It takes a few times before you get it," Beth says. "Try again."

Lisa's second attempt goes much better. Beth's right, she thinks. You can tell where the sweet spot is when you find it. This time, the door stays open.

"There you go. Perfect."

Leslie hands Lisa the plate of chicken, and she and Beth watch as Lisa places it far back into the trap beyond the trip plate.

"Yup. Exactly where it should go," Beth confirms.

Lisa smiles. She's happy to do her part for the striking, unusual dog who's chosen to make his home just a few hundred feet from her own. His story has touched her in a way she's still trying to process.

"One more thing," Beth says. "Wildlife."

"Wildlife?" This hasn't occurred to Lisa.

"The most likely suspects are raccoons and squirrels. Maybe a skunk. I can't remember ever having a coyote or a fox in a trap. They're too smart. Anyway, wildlife needs to be released within two to four hours. Any longer than that, the stress of it can kill them."

Leslie notices the expression on Lisa's face.

"If there's wildlife in the trap, Lisa, just call me. Even if it's the middle of the night. I'll come over and take care of releasing," she says.

"Thanks, Leslie. I'll take you up on that."

"Wonderful." Beth is happy to have that issue, often a sticking point for homeowners who agree to help with the trap, settled. "So. For the first week or so that we have a trap up for a dog like Solomon, we usually don't set it," she continues. "We'll put his food beside the closed trap, set up a trail cam to see how he's reacting. If he doesn't seem bothered by the trap, we'll set it. Sound good?"

Leslie and Lisa nod, pleased to have a plan to recover Solomon in place. But Beth can't help thinking back to Covanta, to Solomon's refusal to go into the trap. Fortunately, they'd had the Gypsy trap and the garage to change things up on him. In her opinion, the darkness and familiarity of the garage had been key, even more crucial than the Gypsy trap itself. They don't have that advantage here. Leslie showed her the ramshackle shed a little while ago. There's no way the Gypsy trap will fit into that tight, crowded space. Unless they come up with some better but currently unimagined plan, this is it. So, probably better to throw some positive energy at it than dwell on Solomon's past behavior.

"Alright. Fingers crossed, let's see what happens. Who knows, maybe this time we'll get really, really lucky."

"We're going to get him," Leslie says. "I have this feeling he ended up in Hull Village for a reason, and that we're somehow part of that reason."

Lisa knows exactly what Leslie means.

The following week is uneventful. Solomon discovers the food placed by the trap and is now coming regularly to Lisa's yard to eat. She's sure he's eating elsewhere, too; Leslie has gotten several phone calls from an employee at Jo's Nautical Bar. He's seen Solomon on the beach eating dead fish, crabs, and the occasional seagull, and taking post-lunch naps on the sand beneath the restaurant's deck. There's also an excellent chance he's pulling trash out of their dumpster, which is low and easily accessible.

Lisa is initially surprised that he's doing those things when he has such good, healthy food to eat at her place. And he doesn't even have to work for it. All he has to do is show up. But the more she thinks about it, the more she wonders if, because of his previous indiscriminate eating, he has worms. She begins putting more food on his plastic plate.

Finally, Beth and Leslie decide it's time to activate the trap. The trail cam photos have regularly shown Solomon walking up to the trap, devouring his food, and moving on. Beth drives down to Hull Village from Newton for the occasion, and she and Leslie sit in the car outside Lisa's house. The car is parked in the late afternoon sun, and the air inside feels uncomfortably warm. But they don't want to roll down the windows. Not even a crack.

"He'll smell us," Beth says. "Absolutely."

And so they sit and wait, eyes focused on the trap, for what seems an eternity. But suddenly he's there, arriving from an unexpected direction. They watch, holding their breath, as he approaches the trap. Once he's right up beside it, it's clear he knows something about the set-up is different. The food is obviously inside the trap instead of outside it, but it seems to Leslie he's noticing more than just that.

"Look at him. He looks like he's inspecting the trap," Leslie whispers.

They watch him walk slowly around the trap's perimeter, sniffing and observing. He's methodical in his inspection, as if trying to figure out exactly how this thing that now holds his food is constructed, how it works.

"That's exactly what he's doing. Clearly, this dog doesn't forget anything. He knows if he goes in there, he's not getting out."

It's precisely what Beth hoped *wouldn't* happen. But there it is. They watch, mesmerized, as Solomon continues his examination of the trap. He stares into it, seeming to note the location of the food, the lift of the trip plate. He looks at the location of the door, at the hinges. Beth is sure he sees it all, every last detail, including the fact that while the front is open, the back is closed.

"The funny thing is, even though he's wary of the trap, he seems really confident," Leslie says. "It's like he's thinking to himself 'I'm hungry, and I'd like some food, so let me check this out and see what it's about. See how I can get what I need.' I think he totally believes in his ability to figure it all out, to get what he needs without putting himself in danger."

"Yup. He wouldn't have survived on his own for this long without that combination of wariness and confidence, that ability to problem-solve."

They sit in silence for the next five minutes, watching Solomon, waiting to see what his next move will be. Finally, he approaches the trap, walks right up to the very edge.

"This is it," Beth whispers. "Get ready."

Standing just outside the trap's open door, Solomon stares inside. The smell of the food holds him there, his mouth moist with saliva, his stomach pinching. He takes one more small step forward, then stops. In that moment his survival instincts kick in, pushing aside his hunger. He turns abruptly away from the trap. Then he heads briskly across the yard, down the wooded path past Ella's playhouse, and disappears from view.

Nine

Hull Village, Massachusetts: April 2012

In the quiet of the morning's wee hours, Solomon twitches and whines, paws flicking up and down. The motion of his dream startles him awake, and he jerks his head up. A quick darting of his eyes around the shed confirms his sole presence inside it. Ears turned outward, he listens for nearby noises. After a time of hearing nothing, he lays his head back down on the drafty floor, muscles relaxing. As he sinks back into sleep Solomon has no idea that, in the yellow house on the hill behind him, the woman who lives there is lying awake, too. That she's thinking about him. Or that, like him, she's alone: alone in ways that are different from his own aloneness, yet at their heart very much the same.

🐕

Lisa lies in the darkness, unable to sleep. The loneliness that's been choking her for months continues unabated, its weight heavy. But in the silence of early morning there is sometimes epiphany, and in a flash of mental clarity she realizes she can't do it, simply can't stay in her marriage. She'd planned to, for Ella's sake; had thought she could hang in there until Ella turned eighteen. But she views the twelve-plus years leading to that day differently now, understands how large they loom, how excruciatingly lonely. She has to find another path out, a path she has yet to stumble upon.

Staring up at the ceiling, she wonders what it would be like to be Solomon, perfectly capable of leading a solitary existence. She wonders other things about him, too: Is he happy without a family, or does he live on his own because it's all he knows? Is he, like her, afraid of what comes next? Have people he's encountered inflicted trust-impacting wounds to his body or soul? If so, she hopes those wounds can be healed enough for him to find a family to love him, a family he can love back. If that's what he wants, what he's looking for. And for some reason, she can't stop believing it is.

He reminds me of myself, she thinks. We're both on a journey to something new and better, and we're both finding the traveling a bit rough. Who knows? Maybe we can find a way to help each other make it through.

Lisa begins reading books on divorce and children. How to do it right, how to not screw kids up. And in the middle of one of those books something clicks, completely shifting the way she sees her responsibility to Ella. A childhood spent with both parents living in the same house *isn't* the most important thing she owes her child. The most important things she owes Ella are these: The knowledge that mistakes aren't forever. A chance to grow up seeing and understanding what true love looks like, feels like. And the conviction that she should settle for nothing less. Ever. In a world that, from Lisa's perspective, is so messed up when it comes to love and sex—especially for girls—one of her greatest responsibilities as a mother is to give her daughter these gifts.

So she and Dave finally make the decision to split up, begin considering how best to dismantle the years' worth of shared financial commitments that bind them together. Selling homes, buying new ones, moving to another town. Moving on.

"I'm sorry, Dave." Lisa reaches out, touches his hand. He places his own hand over hers.

"Me, too. But I think it's what's best. For all of us."

They start the process of setting their plans in motion. Lisa puts a house she owned previous to their marriage on the market, and they assess what needs to be updated in their jointly owned home before listing it. She loves the big yellow Victorian and will miss it. Still, it's too much for her to keep up alone.

Maintaining forward momentum with regard to the financial and real estate aspects of their impending split is proving relatively easy. But the human factors involved are like a wall they can't seem to avoid running into, a rock solid barrier that slams them to a painful halt. What to tell Ella? When to tell her, and where, and how? Though they discuss these questions at length, they set no definitive time frame. Lisa isn't ready to pull that trigger yet. She needs to be in a better place with the situation herself. Children have a special kind of radar for picking up uncertainty and fear, and she doesn't want Ella tapping into those emotions.

It's not that Lisa is second guessing the decision she and Dave have made, or their plans for moving forward. But, as with most major changes in her life, she needs to sit with it all for a while. Once she's had the chance to do so, to fully process the end of her marriage, she'll be fine. And then it'll be time to tell Ella.

But plans don't always turn out the way they're supposed to. Not long after Lisa and Dave finish hashing things through, their progress hits a major snag. It turns out Dave's recently purchased new house, bought at auction, is going to be a total renovation project. At least a year's worth of work.

"Would it be okay with you if I stay here until the house is finished?" he asks Lisa. "The reno's going to be pricey, and it'd be great if I didn't have to pay rent on top of the reno expenses."

She stares at him for a moment, feels a flush of anger on her cheeks.

"Are you serious, Dave? I mean, it would've been nice if you'd asked me this before you actually bought the house, you know?"

"You're right, I should have. I'm sorry. I just didn't think it was going to need so much work. But it's so perfect…wait'll you see Ella's bedroom!"

Lisa still wishes he'd consulted her before buying the house. But she understands how tough it is to pass up a dream house. And they've already done the hard work of agreeing to divorce. Waiting another year to make it a reality is something she can live with.

"It's fine," she tells him. "But if it'll be more than a year, we're going to need to revisit this."

He gives her a quick hug. "I appreciate it."

"No worries. And Dave? I'm happy you found your perfect house. I really am."

As the last week of April approaches, Team Solomon's frustration with the ongoing trap situation is at its peak. They've tried everything to recover him. Hot rotisserie chicken. Roast beef. French fries, which, according to Hope, Solomon is particularly fond of. And still, he refuses to go into the trap. The waiting is getting old.

Driving home to Newton after another evening of waiting for Solomon and then watching him avoid the food in the trap, Beth has a long conversation with herself. Clearly, they're not going to be able to recover this dog using a trap. At least not without some Covanta-esque trickery, which they're not set up for in Hull Village. She's been hoping he might give in one of these times, might take a risk for a particularly enticing meal. But no dice.

In her opinion, they need to come up with a new-to-Solomon plan, something that doesn't require a trap. They're going to need help figuring something out, though; at this point, her own bag of tricks is empty. When she arrives home, she calls Alan Borgal at the Animal Rescue League in Boston. If there's one person in the rescue and recovery world who might be smarter than Solomon, she thinks, it's Alan.

The new plan for Solomon's recovery has been discussed for days, passed veterinary scrutiny, and is now ready to be put into action. They're going to dart him. It's an option both complex and risky. Still, with careful planning and execution, the risks can be minimized to the extent that in this case, everyone considers them worth taking. Once they have him, Hope Cruser at Underhound Railroad will bring him back to Maine and foster him herself. Everything's in place. Now they just need to recover him.

On an early afternoon in the last week of April, Beth, Leslie, and Alan convene in Hull Village. Beth has enlisted a few experienced volunteers, and Alan has brought along his ARL colleagues Brian and Bill. Alan would have preferred to have more people involved, more bodies to cover the various routes Solomon might travel throughout the afternoon. But in a situation like this, with the combination of a highly intelligent dog and the potential for things to go wrong, less was going to have to be more.

The day is sunny and brisk, with a wind blowing off the ocean. Despite the possible complications the wind brings to the darting plan, Beth has a good feeling about their chances: it's her birthday, and the gift to end all gifts would be recovering Solomon. It's going to happen. She's sure of it.

The group huddles together in Hull Cemetery, going over plans and details. Who's doing what, how they'll approach a variety of situations that may occur, how they'll communicate with each other. There's a current of energy and anticipation running through everyone. They remind Beth of a special operations team, all jazzed for their mission.

"Okay, everybody, listen up," Alan says. "We gotta cover as much area as possible. If a dog's darted near water, that's where they always head. Right to the water. I don't know why, they just do. If Solomon makes it to the water, he's gonna drown. So we need to head him off before he gets there."

He assigns each person a section of the large, circular buffer zone between the water and the area where Leslie and Beth believe Solomon's home base is located. Two volunteers will be stationed along the seawall. Another will be parked near the water on the south side, closer to the causeway leading into Hull Village. Beth's assigned parking spot is a bit up the street from that volunteer, along the side of the road. Leslie will be in the ACO van on the west side, and Brian hiding between some parked cars not too far from Alan and Bill.

"How will we know he's been darted?" one of the volunteers asks Alan.

"I'll let Brian know over the walkie-talkie, then he'll call you. Make sure he has your cell number. At that point I'll probably have a pretty good idea of what direction Solomon's heading in so you can all move to that area."

"Okay."

"Another thing. You gotta keep an eye on the street, make sure he doesn't get hit after he's darted."

Beth wonders if everyone's gut feels as queasy as hers does right now. Probably, she thinks. This is a highly orchestrated plan with even higher stakes, and no one wants to be the reason it fails.

"I'll be hiding between some parked cars with the dart gun. When I see him go by, if I can get a clear shot at him, I'll shoot. Bill will be somewhere near me with a hand net, see if we can net him before he gets too far. Anybody got any questions?"

No one does.

"All right then. Let's go get our boy!"

Beth needs to stretch her legs and clear her mind. She climbs onto the seawall and faces the ocean, hands shoved into the pockets of her jacket, the wind whipping her hair wildly about. What began as an organized plan has, within less than two hours, devolved into something just short of chaos. For some crazy reason, they've been operating under the belief that Solomon's going to just trot on over, oblivious to the unfamiliar scents surrounding him. He's going to saunter right by the cars where Alan's crouched with a dart gun, and boom! Darted. If only, she thinks. Instead, Solomon has them all spinning in circles.

Part of the problem, she knows, is that it's obvious from their presence that something unusual is happening in the neighborhood. Curious residents approach, ask what they're doing, what's going on. When she explains that they're trying to recover a missing dog living in the neighborhood, everyone knows exactly which dog she's talking about.

"Is it the big black and white dog? I see him all the time. He's awesome!"

"The black and white dog, right? The one who looks like a cow? I just saw him, right up the street, like two minutes ago. Want me to go get him for you?"

"No! Thanks, but no. We need you to just ignore him, let him come to us. We don't want to spook him or make him leave the area. We appreciate everyone wanting to help. But the best way to help is to call the Hull ACO if you see him. We have a recovery plan, but it's not going to work if we have people chasing him."

Beth doesn't mention that the plan consists of a man hiding between some cars, waiting to shoot the dog with a dart gun. She doesn't want people engaging in this situation any more than they already are, and the novelty of the darting might make disengagement impossible. Fortunately, no one asks how they're actually planning to recover Solomon. They just want to know what's going on.

Even so, the presence of so many people congregating in the area is making the plan significantly more difficult to carry out. The breeze off the water has kicked up. She worries that the scent of everyone gathered at the seawall is drifting up to the hilly part of the neighborhood, where Solomon's most likely hanging out. If it reaches him, that'll be it. He won't go anywhere near Alan's hiding place, and they'll have to shut down the operation and go home without the dog. Again.

Solomon strolls along the small beach near the Coast Guard station, returning from a scavenging trip to Jo's Nautical Bar. He trots across the sand and onto the sidewalk, walking until he nears the intersection of Ocean Avenue and Main Street. Suddenly he stops, lifts his nose to the air. He smells something different, detects unusual activity in the area. A sense of anxiety hangs in the air, and he picks up on it immediately.

Now he, too, is anxious, and he steps up his pace, heading toward the safety of his shed.

But as he heads toward Main Street, a strong gust of wind off the ocean carries a tangle of human scents in his direction. Most are unfamiliar, but in the mixture he isolates and recognizes three. Desperate to get away from the source of those scents, he races frantically across busy streets and up and down hills, searching for safety.

Solomon is onto them. Leslie's cell phone buzzes incessantly, inundated with calls from neighborhood residents aware of the recovery effort. It seems Solomon's doing a loop between the parking lot of the Methodist church on Spring Street and the area up over the hill near Newton Street. *Crap.* This is turning into a circus, and they—Team Solomon—are the clowns. She should've known this would go sideways. Too complicated, too many ways it could be screwed up. One of those plans that sounds great in theory, but in actual practice? Not so much.

As she sits behind the wheel of the parked van, poised for the next call, Solomon appears. He's running along the opposite sidewalk, heading in her direction. It's the first time she's seen him since arriving at her assigned spot. And what she sees alarms her. She's observed him, on more than one occasion, stop and look both ways before crossing the street. But now she watches him veer off the sidewalk and tear across the street as if pursued by demons, oblivious to potential danger. This is not good, she thinks. Not at all. He's not only onto them, he's running spooked. She grabs her cell phone and calls Alan.

Alan crouches between the cars, dart gun ready, knees aching. This isn't going as he'd hoped. Solomon is just too damn smart. Alan had made a trip to the area a few days earlier to scope things out. He wanted to see exactly what they'd be dealing with, get a better sense of the stretch of coastline and marshes. Now he begins to worry the dog may know too many short-cuts to the water for them to safely cover if they do manage to dart him.

And to top it all off, after a call from Brian and another couple from Leslie, it looks like Solomon's onto the fact that something out of the ordinary's going on in his environment and he's running scared. The last thing Alan wants is for Solomon to run across the street and get hit. Based on his last conversation with Leslie, it seems like this outcome is becoming more and more of a possibility.

"Dammit to hell," he mutters. Nothing has worked in their favor today. The strong sea breeze, the curious residents, the lack of a clear shot angle, and the intelligence of a dog who continues to elude them. All these factors have coalesced to turn what he thought would be a successful plan into something they no longer have control over. He hates to give up on it, but for Solomon's safety, it's time to shut things down.

Instinctively, Solomon does not return to his shed. Instead, he runs a loop of hills and streets, runs until he's exhausted. He finally settles into a new hiding place, beneath the porch of a summer home on Andrew Avenue. Located in a hilly area, it's a good distance from the ocean, from the anxiety and disturbing scents he'd detected there.

Lying on top of hard dirt, back pressed tightly against the cold cement of the home's foundation, Solomon's heart pounds. His ears are straight up and turned outward, listening for footsteps, for voices. But there is nothing. Eventually, darkness falls. He hears nothing but the wetland peepers, detects no scent in the air but salt and moist earth. Unable to stand in the space, he wiggles across the packed dirt, dried leaves and tiny twigs and rough pebbles scratching the vulnerable skin of his belly. He pokes his head out into the fresh air. His shoulders emerge next, and then the rest of his body. Solomon shakes himself once—a good, hard shake—then heads off into the night, making his way quickly and quietly to his shed.

Ten

Hull Village, Massachusetts: April–June 2012

Shutting down the darting operation is demoralizing for Team Solomon. Their investment of physical and emotional energy had been total, their hopes of recovering him stratospherically high. Now, back at the emotional lows of square one, they work to devise yet another plan. What is it going to take to bring this extraordinary dog to safety? At this point, the answer to that question is a mystery. A mystery without a single clue.

Though not directly involved in the darting attempt, Lisa is as disappointed as everyone else by its failure. Her connection with Solomon grows stronger with each trip out to the trap to replenish his food and water. She worries about him constantly. On the rare day she doesn't see him traveling through her yard, she experiences a sense of panic abated only by his reappearance.

It's not that she *wants* to love him. She doesn't. It feels too dangerous, the number of terrible things that could happen to him as he goes about the daily business of surviving too many. Yet somehow, he's managed to get under her skin. Is it the distraction he provides from her own troubles? The existential similarities of their respective situations? Or is it something else, something much deeper? She's not sure. Not yet.

What she is sure of is that if he were gone, she'd miss him. Truly and deeply miss him. Even so, she hopes the next attempt to recover him, whatever it is, will be successful. Without this step, it seems there's no way for him to have the happy life she wishes for him.

Solomon trots away from the shed, using his shortcut. Up the path, past the playhouse, across the yard to the street. He crosses the street, cuts across two yards going uphill, and arrives at a newly discovered source of food. The food appears in the small front yard of a large white house. He's recently found a hiding place beneath the porch of that house, and now he wiggles his way through its opening and waits, stomach rumbling, for the sound of footsteps on the floorboards above him and the smell of food.

Solomon has dozed off when footsteps moving above his head wake him. He squiggles over to the opening beneath the porch, watches the woman's feet travel to a large tree. The feet turn, move toward him, then pass above him once again before their sound disappears. He waits to be sure the footsteps don't return, then shimmies out from beneath the porch and trots over to the tree. His head turns left, right, his ears at attention, scanning for anything indicating danger. Satisfied with the situation, he drops his head and eats, licking every bit of food off the plate. The food is good, and there's enough of it to quiet his stomach. He runs his tongue over his nose then ambles off in the direction of the beach, tail wagging.

There's one piece of good news in the immediate aftermath of the aborted darting: Solomon hasn't been spooked out of the area. Leslie receives regular sighting calls from Hull Village, as well as from areas a bit farther south, in Hull proper. Solomon has been seen at the Fort, up in the Newton Street neighborhood, and down near the marshes. He's also been hanging around a couple of restaurants at the quieter end of

Paragon Park. One caller says she saw him pulling a trash bag apart over by the dumpster in the parking lot behind one of the restaurants.

The Paragon Park sightings initially have Leslie biting her nails. They're south of his usual hangouts, and south is the only way out of Hull. On land, anyway. She wonders if Solomon is planning his exit to wherever he's headed next. But the fact that he continues to return to the Newton Street area tells her he feels settled there. Settled enough that even the chaos of the darting day hasn't pushed him out and onward. We got lucky this time, she thinks.

It takes a few days for everyone to digest the disappointment of the darting attempt. Leslie and Beth communicate daily, tossing around ideas, trying to figure out what to do next. The trap is still set in Lisa's yard, and she continues to leave food out beside it for Solomon. But according to Lisa, his eating schedule seems off.

"Interesting. I think someone's feeding him," Beth tells Leslie.

Leslie agrees. "I'll do some asking around the neighborhood, see if I can figure out what's going on."

It turns out she doesn't need to do any sleuthing at all. The following day, she receives a call from a woman on Andrew Avenue, about a big black and white dog hanging out under her porch. A dog she's very kindly been putting food and water out for.

"I don't mind him being under there. I just thought you should know, in case anyone calls you looking for him."

"I really appreciate your call. I'm aware of the dog, and I'm working with the ARL and some other people to recover him."

"Oh, that's good to hear."

"How long have you been seeing him around?" Leslie asks.

"Maybe a week? Maybe a little longer. I'm not a hundred percent sure."

Well, this is an interesting development, Leslie thinks. So he has what may be a second home base, along with a second source of good food. Gotta hand it to him. Smart *and* opportunistic.

"Would you mind if I stop by to poke around?"

"Not at all. I'm home pretty much all day today."

"Perfect. I'll be over in an hour or so. And I know this probably sounds harsh, but we need you to stop feeding him. He needs to be hungry if we're ever going to be able to trap him."

When Leslie arrives, a middle-aged woman is waiting for her on the porch. Her smile as she waves to Leslie is warm, kind. It's uncanny, Leslie thinks, Solomon's ability to gravitate toward places where kind people live or work. And not just your run-of-the-mill kind people, either. He's drawn to a specific type of kind people, the type who notice and go out of their way to help a needy dog. It's a survival skill, to be sure. But it's one she considers more complex than a dog's typical survival skills, a sort of sophisticated blend of cognitive and instinctual.

The woman walks down the porch steps to meet Leslie.

The home, like many in Hull Village, is a large Victorian, with a front porch spanning the width of the house. The front yard is small, but the side yard is large and flat, with a good amount of space separating it from the neighboring house. Leslie makes a mental note to speak with the people who live in that house, too, about not feeding him.

"Let me show you around the yard," the woman offers.

"Thanks, that'd be great."

She leads Leslie over to the far end of the porch, the end closest to the house next door, and points to a small opening hidden by bushes.

"Right there. That's how he gets in and out."

Leslie looks at the opening, then at the woman.

"You've gotta be kidding."

"I know. It's small. But somehow, he manages to squeeze through it."

Small is an understatement. The width of the opening is more than enough for a dog of Solomon's size. But the height? Leslie estimates the space to be six or seven inches high, about the height of a stair step. And it's the same height all the way back to the foundation. He'd have to squiggle in on his belly and then remain in that position, because there's nowhere near enough overhead space for him to stand.

Is this where he sleeps, then? Is the shed in the yard behind Lisa's house only his day-time shelter? It makes sense that he'd feel less exposed under a porch than in the shed. And a low, tight space makes it easier for him to benefit from his own body heat in the still-cool nights near the ocean.

But to not be able to stand without leaving the space? That might be a deal-breaker. Maybe this is just a regular napping place, as opposed to a legitimate home base. There's no way to know for sure, but if this is a secondary home base, she can't help wondering how many more there might be. Is she going to have to set and monitor trail cams and traps all over Hull Village?

"Do you think he's under there right now?" she asks the woman.

"No. He's usually only here mornings and early evenings."

Leslie kneels down close to the opening beneath the porch and shines her phone's flashlight into the darkness. No sign of him, but she notices two small areas of loose, dark dirt dug from around the opening. Taking a closer look, she sees that the digging has made the entrance to the space much deeper than it appears from the outside. He has plenty of head room to slither in and out. The space is safe, quiet, completely hidden from view. It's a perfect place to sleep, or to slip into if he needs a quick hiding place in this part of the neighborhood.

She stands, brushes the dirt off the legs of her jeans.

"Well, this looks like a great place for him to hang out. It's good that he's comfortable here, but like I said, we need you to stop feeding him. Do you think the people in the house next door might be feeding him, too?"

"I don't know. Probably not. The man who lives there is blind, so I'd guess he's not aware of the dog. But you never know, I suppose."

"Well, I'll go over and chat with him, just in case. Nice to meet you. And thanks again for your time."

The woman shakes Leslie's outstretched hand. She hopes the ACO is able to catch the dog soon, because it's going to break her heart to not feed him. She's always fed the hungry, human or animal, ever since she was a child. Ignoring a hungry dog goes against everything she believes in, everything she is. But if that's what it's going to take to recover the dog, whose name she now knows is Solomon, well, she'll just have to do it. She'll put her heart back together later, when he's safe and living in a warm, dry home with a loving family.

Leslie cuts across the lawn separating the two houses. Before walking up the steps onto the porch she glances at the wooden latticework, looking for breaks. Or holes dug in the dirt. Everything appears intact. It's unlikely Solomon's hanging out under this porch, but she'll need to check out the sides to be sure. If there's one thing she's learned from this dog, it's to never make assumptions.

She presses the doorbell and waits. There's a lot of barking on the other side of the door, but nothing else. Maybe the man's not home. She's just about to give the doorbell another ring when she hears footsteps approaching the door.

"Who is it?" a man's voice asks.

"Hello, sir. I'm Leslie Badger, the Hull Animal Control Officer. I'd like to talk with you about a missing dog who's settled into this neighborhood. Do you have a few minutes?"

The barking on the other side of the door continues, and Leslie hears the man talking to the dog. His voice is reassuring, gentle. When the barking stops, the door opens and the man and his dog walk out onto the porch. Like his next-door neighbor, he's older, polite and soft-spoken. He gestures toward the cozy seating area set up in a corner of the porch.

"Please, sit down. I'm happy to speak with you."

And so they sit, Leslie relating Solomon's story, the man listening with interest while running his hand lightly along the dog's head resting on his knee. The dog's eyes are closed, her expression blissful. It must be heaven to be this man's dog, Leslie thinks. She wants so much to help give Solomon the opportunity to be this cherished someday. When she finishes her story, the man offers one of his own.

"I believe I may have petted Solomon a little while ago."

Leslie is stunned. She can't imagine anything this man could have said that would shock her more. Someone actually touching Solomon? Highly unlikely. To the best of her knowledge, no one has touched Solomon unless he was in their home or in a shelter. Still, she's curious to hear the rest of the man's story.

"Where did this happen?" she asks.

"Right here on the porch. I was sitting in my chair, just like I am now, with my dog. She barked a couple times and started to whine. Then I heard light footsteps coming up the porch stairs, across the porch to where we were sitting. I figured it was probably a dog. There's a few people in this neighborhood who don't obey the leash law, and for some reason their dogs seem to end up on my porch. Anyway, my dog growled once. After that everything was quiet. And then I felt the weight of a head on my lap. It was heavy, and I knew it wasn't my own dog. I reached out and petted the dog's head. He stood there like that for a few minutes while I petted his head and his side. Then he walked back down the steps and left."

"Did he ever come back?"

"No. That was it."

"Is there anything else you can tell me about the dog?"

"Well, I can't tell you what color he is, or much about what he looks like, or even if he's really a 'he.' I thought 'he' because the dog's big, but I could be wrong. What I *can* tell you is that his coat's very short, his head's angular and broad, his ears stand up, he's tall, and he's in good shape. No ribs poking out on his sides. He's what I call sturdy. That sound like it might be him?"

"Very much so."

"I can tell you something else about him, too. And I guess this is probably going to sound like some crackpot thing to say, but I'm going to say it anyway. When he came up onto the porch, I felt some kind of a presence. I can't really describe it. Just something calming, quieting. And when he left it was gone. If it's him, I hope you catch him. Because that's one heck of a special dog."

"He is, for sure. And none of that sounds crackpot to me. To be honest, I know exactly what you mean about his presence," Leslie says. "If he happens to come back, or starts hanging around your porch, please don't feed him. I know it sounds cruel, but we need him to be hungry if we're going to be able to trap him."

"You got it."

Pulling away from the curb, Leslie's already calling Beth. Probably time to Favorite this one, she thinks. More looking at the road, less looking at the numbers on her screen.

Beth picks up with her usual greeting. "Leslie!"

"Okay, you're never going to believe this. Solomon went up onto a blind man's porch and let the man pet him."

Beth is sure she's heard wrong. "Start over."

"Solomon went up onto a blind man's porch, and he let the man pet him."

"Are you serious? Holy shit. How did you find this out?"

Leslie recounts the day's events, from the woman's phone call to the conversation with the man on his porch.

"So in a nutshell, Solomon has another possible home base, and the woman who's feeding him is going to stop," Leslie says.

"And he went up to a blind man and let himself be petted."

Yes. There was that, too.

"Knowing that makes me die a little inside," Beth goes on. "Obviously, it's wonderful that he actually approached someone and let himself be touched. Now we know he hasn't become completely human-averse. But what kills me is that, of all the people he could've approached, he chose the one person who has no idea who he is. The one person who won't recognize him and try to catch him. Because the man's probably the only person in Hull Village who hasn't seen a single goddamn flyer! I've dealt with some very smart dogs over the years, but Solomon's on a completely different level. It's ridiculous."

She doesn't want to say it aloud—not yet, anyway—but she's beginning to think there's a very good chance Solomon's going to beat them at their own game. Yes, they've failed to recover other dogs. But in most of those cases, it was because they were never able to pin down the dog's location. Those still-missing dogs remain on her mind, and she continues to compare found dogs and new sightings with GSDR's "Missing" flyers. "Never give up" is her motto.

But Solomon's situation is different. For now, his traveling days appear to be on pause. They know exactly where he is. This recovery should, theoretically, be relatively easy. Yet so far, it's been anything but. And every time she learns of another indicator of Solomon's extreme intelligence, her expectation that things will soon swing in their favor diminishes.

"It's completely ridiculous," Leslie agrees. "I've never seen a dog like this in my life."

Trying to recover Solomon has, in many ways, put a different spin on almost everything Leslie knows about the process. She now realizes that if she wants to successfully bring him to safety, she's going to have to start thinking more like a dog and less like a person. So far, the species shift has been challenging.

By the early days of June, it's clear Solomon has no plans to go into the trap. On shot after shot taken by the trail camera, he approaches the trap, sniffs at the food inside, and continues on his way.

"So now what?" Leslie asks Beth. The idea of Solomon living outside on his own through another winter is one she can't accept. Even though it's only the second week of June, she feels a sense of desperation when she contemplates what the future might hold for this dog who's become—she might as well admit it—her obsession.

Beth is silent on the other end of the phone, then sighs.

"Let me call Alan, see if he's got anything else up his sleeve. I doubt he's going to want to try the darting again. But maybe a drop-net, if there's a good place to set one up."

Leslie is familiar with the principle of a drop-net, but has never seen one set up.

"What makes a good place to set it?"

"Someplace open, good amount of space on either side. Flat. Easily accessible. Once the net's dropped you have to get to it immediately. Ideally, the dog gets tangled up a bit in the net. But that doesn't always happen. And if it doesn't, the dog can get out if he's quick and smart."

Like Solomon, Leslie thinks.

"It takes a while to get it set up, and I know the ARL uses it pretty much as a last resort type of thing," Beth continues. "We'll see what Alan says, but I think we're officially at the last resort stage. Unless he can come up with another idea. I know I'm stumped."

"Me, too."

"So. I'll call Alan, and if you can scout out a few possible locations for the net, that'd be great."

Leslie doesn't think she needs to do much scouting. She already has a place in mind that, based on Beth's description, seems perfect.

"There's a section of open yard between the house where Solomon's hanging out under the porch and the blind man's house that could work. I'm not sure which house that yard belongs to, but I'll find out. It's large, open, flat, and you can see it right from the street. Which may not be a good thing from Solomon's perspective, I guess. But maybe lack of privacy won't be an issue for him, since the net would be set up in an area where he's already comfortable."

Maybe, maybe not. No way to predict. Not with this dog. But privacy issue aside, the location Leslie's proposing sounds spot on to Beth.

"Can you text me a picture of that area? I'll shoot it over to Alan, see what he thinks."

"Yeah, sure. I should be able to get over there later this afternoon. And while I'm there, I'll find out who the yard belongs to and ask if they're okay with having a drop-net set on it."

Leslie stands on the sidewalk in front of the expanse of yard between the two houses on Andrew Avenue, aiming her phone's camera. Left shot, center, right. Photos taken, she walks up the steps of the house with the porch she now refers to as Solomon's porch, and rings the bell.

The door is opened by the same woman she spoke with before, and after a brief conversation Leslie has the permission they need. She taps her Photos icon, selects the last three pictures, texts them to Beth. Leslie has barely reached the end of the street after sending the text when her phone rings.

"Leslie! Perfect spot. Do we have permission to set?"

"Yeah, we're good to go."

"Fab. I'm going to send these to Alan now, get his input. I'll let you know when I hear from him."

Beth hangs up, takes a look at the still unchecked items on the day's to-do list. A conversation with Alan can last two hours, sometimes more. As fond as she is of him, that man can talk longer than anyone she's ever known. Tangent upon winding tangent that, eventually, weave themselves together into something that makes perfect, beautiful, brilliant sense. She figures she can complete the remaining items on her list in about an hour and a half, and then she'll be free for the rest of the day. Plenty of time for a chat with Alan, no matter how many directions the conversation spins off into. In the meantime, she texts him Leslie's photos of the potential drop-net location.

Beth's conversation with Alan turns out to be surprisingly short. He must be snowed under, she thinks. She gives him a rundown of the situation in Hull Village. He agrees that the drop-net's probably the only way they're going to recover Solomon. The area between the two houses, he thinks, looks perfect. He figures he can get himself, Brian, and Bill over to Hull Village to get the net set up sometime in the next ten days.

"Not making any promises; there's a lot going on," he tells Beth.

"There's that cruelty case we're working on, the hoarder case out in central Mass, and then all the other stuff that just pops up outta nowhere. But I think we should be able to get out there in the next week and a half. Maybe a little sooner if we catch a break with everything else. In the meantime, Leslie needs to start feeding Solomon in the exact place we're gonna set the net."

"Great. Thanks, Alan. As always, you're the best."

Beth calls Leslie to fill her in on her conversation with Alan, then plops onto her sofa, a dog snuggled close on either side of her. She picks up the book she's currently reading and is soon absorbed in the doings of its characters—not one of whom is being constantly, relentlessly, mercilessly outsmarted by a dog.

Eleven

Leslie sits cross-legged at the edge of the yard on Andrew Avenue, waiting for Alan and his ARL colleagues Brian and Bill. She checks her watch. They should have arrived nearly half an hour ago. Probably stuck in traffic. She closes her eyes, breathing summer into her lungs, grateful for the sun's light and heat on her bare limbs. This kind of perfect summer day is one of the many reasons she lives in New England. Her thoughts drift aimlessly, an infrequent freedom, until the slamming of a car door snaps her eyes open. She gets up, brushes bits of grass and earth off her butt, and walks over to the van. Time to get this show cranking.

Alan opens the van's rear doors and he, Bill, and Brian momentarily disappear inside. They re-emerge looking like the three wise men, bearing gifts of plastic or metal. A plastic case. A black metal box with an antenna on top and wires protruding from the bottom that Leslie assumes is some kind of receiver. A long, rounded-oblong white box, and a hammer substantial enough to do some serious demo work.

"Anything I can grab?" Leslie asks.

"Nope, I think we're good," Alan says, reaching out with his free hand to close up the van. "Alright. Let's get this thing set up."

They lug their plastic and metal across the grass and drop it all in the middle of the yard. Bill opens the case, then extricates poles, stakes, ropes, a net, and four metal pipe-like gadgets with wires poking from the top of each side. Leslie positions herself close enough to observe what's going on, but far enough to stay out of the way. Beth was right, she thinks. Based on what she's seen so far, the set-up for a drop-net is indeed complicated and time-consuming, even with three people. She wonders if one person could do it alone in a pinch. With a lot of previous set-up experience, she imagines it might be possible. But it would be slow going.

And does it come with instructions? She supposes it must, but if so, they're not being used. She figures these guys can probably do the set-up in their sleep. And besides, what guy looks at instructions for anything? No one she knows. She, on the other hand, is a big fan of the step-by-step.

"Does the net come with set-up instructions?" she asks.

"Yeah. They also have a pretty good video on YouTube. After you set it up once, though, you don't really need instructions," Alan says.

Maybe if you're Alan Borgal or Brian O'Connor you don't, Leslie thinks. But she's pretty sure she'll be keeping the instructions handy if the town of Hull ever decides to purchase a drop-net for her. In reality, Solomon's more likely to waltz up and allow himself to be escorted into the ARL van than she is to get a drop-net. Still, she's glad to be able to observe the process. These guys are the best at what they do, and she'll learn things she won't learn from a set of instructions or a YouTube video.

Before they lay out the net, Brian and Bill do a slow walk around the yard, eyes scanning the ground. The net is twenty-five feet by twenty-five feet, and a corresponding area has to be completely free of any debris. From Leslie's vantage point the ground appears clear. Brian, though, finds a few twigs lying around that have to go, as well as a handful of pebbles. To Leslie, they seem too small to be problematic.

"Why do you need to remove such tiny pebbles and twigs?" she asks.

"The net has to lie flat on the ground, before we set it and after we drop it. You can't leave anything on the ground, even something small, that could tear a hole in the net or hurt the dog when he's tangled up in it," Brian explains.

"Makes sense," Leslie says. No point in dropping a net that might rip and allow the dog beneath it to escape. It's also an expensive piece of equipment. Definitely not something a non-profit organization is going to be happy about having to replace.

The space in the middle of the yard is now cleared. Leslie watches the three men lay the square net flat on the ground, stretching it on all sides.

"Looks like there's still some center drag in there," Alan says. "Pull that side over in the back up some more. A little more, square it up ... yeah, okay. Looks good."

The net now stretched completely flat, Brian scoops up the pile of long metal poles and carries them back to the net.

"How high are those poles?" Leslie asks.

"Eight feet. You want to have enough headroom under the net for a dog to feel comfortable going in and out. A net this size doesn't have a center pole, so the middle sinks a little. Eight-foot poles keep that part high enough that the net doesn't touch the dog."

"Got it."

Leslie takes a closer look at everything laid out on the grass alongside the net. There's a twelve-volt wireless receiver powered by a battery, and a five-amp remote control that both powers and kills the net. She reads the word "watertight" on the receiver. That's good, because even if it doesn't rain, the moist, salt-saturated air in Hull Village can do some serious damage to electrical components.

Each eight-foot pole is actually a set of two four-foot poles with internal connecting sleeves, one half fitting tightly over the other. Along with the poles, there are four short stakes and four additional, pole-like stakes; four ropes; and four carabiners. There are also the four tube-like pieces with wires sticking out of each side that she'd noticed when Bill had first opened the plastic case. She assumes those must slide over the top of each pole and connect to the net. It's all quite impressive and ingenious.

Brian and Alan begin putting the poles together. Bill gets to work squaring up and hammering the first of the longer stakes into the ground behind each corner of the net.

"Alan, grab me one of those sleeves," Brian says.

He takes the slender metal tube from Alan, inserts it into the bottom half of the pole, and fits the top half firmly over it. Then he brings the pole over to the stake Bill has driven in. Alan ambles over carrying one of the small metal pipes with the wires on top.

"What's that, Alan?" Leslie asks.

"Combination of a release harness and a side volt. They've got electro-magnets in them, and when the power to the net's cut, the net's released."

She watches as Brian holds the pole almost parallel to the ground while Alan slides the release harness over the top and tightens it.

"You wanna get this right at about six feet for a dog Solomon's size," Alan continues. "And you wanna make sure you don't make it too tight, or you'll bend the pole."

Duly noted.

Brian threads one of the ropes through a slot on one end of the release harness, then pulls the pole vertical and sets it onto the stake.

"So what we're gonna do now is pull this guy rope back and attach it to one of the guy stakes. Make sure each corner of the net's stabilized," Alan explains.

Bill pounds the guy stake into the ground at a forty-five-degree angle, and Brian attaches the rope to it. The first corner set-up is complete.

The process is repeated three more times. Leslie accompanies Bill and Brian from corner to corner, observing closely, attempting to visually memorize the steps.

The team stands back from the net to survey their work.

"Looks good," Alan says.

"So what happens from here?" Leslie asks him.

"We'll keep feeding him in the same spot where he's been eating. But now that spot's under the center of the net, so it might take him some time to get used to it. We'll see. Once he starts eating regularly under the net we'll come down, activate it, and sit in the van 'til it's time to drop it."

"So you'll be right there when it drops?"

"Yup. You gotta be able to get to it in thirty seconds or less. If you don't, and the dog isn't fully tangled in it, he can escape. If a dog escapes from under a downed net, he's never going under it again. You get one chance with this, so you gotta make sure you don't blow it."

One chance. Holy crap, Leslie thinks. No pressure or anything.

"Start mixing his food with some broth," Alan goes on. "We want him under the center of the net for as long as possible, with his head down. It'll take him longer to eat if his food's soupy."

Before heading back to Boston, the ARL team moves the trail camera from its place near the net to a new spot with a wider range of visibility.

"Alright, I think we're done here," Brian says, after checking the camera's angle one last time. "Hopefully, we'll be back down in a week or so to drop this thing and finally get our boy."

Hopefully. Leslie likes that choice of words. Hopeful. Full of hope. As she takes a last admiring look at the drop-net and the promise it holds, it's the perfect description of how she feels.

Solomon walks purposefully along Andrew Avenue toward the yard where he finds food. A while ago, the human stopped leaving food for him by the tree. He no longer sees or smells food in or beside the long metal box, either. The only food is in an open area close to the porch he sometimes naps under during the day. This is where he heads now. When he arrives, he stops short, pulls his ears back. There are tall, slender objects placed in the area surrounding the plate of food, which is now under something large, see-through. And there are scents. Human scents. Scents he recognizes, associates with frightening experiences.

He stands a distance from the food, sniffing the air and ground, listening for the sound of voices and footsteps. After a short time, his senses confirm the humans are no longer in the area. He moves to the bowl, eats quickly, and leaves even more quickly than that.

Leslie settles in at her kitchen table and opens her laptop, popping in the SD card she pulled from the trail camera at the net. She scrolls through frame after frame: Solomon approaching the yard. Solomon circling around to the back of the net, walking under it and straight over to the bright yellow bowl under dead center. Solomon, head bent over the bowl, devouring every last morsel of food. He leaves nothing behind, ever. She knows this because she's the one feeding him. The one crawling under the net twice a day, awkwardly making her way, crouched like a human crab, to the center of the net to replace his food.

Watching his behavior and movements on her laptop screen feels very intimate to her. It's a one-sided intimacy, but it's the best way she can think of to describe her feelings as she looks at those camera shots. Still frames taken when he thought he was alone, unobserved. The whole thing has something of the element of spying on someone, of catching glimpses of true self.

In the ten or so weeks since Solomon has taken up residence in Hull Village, Leslie has developed an abiding affection for him. Which, she has to admit, has taken her more than a bit by surprise. She cares about all the animals she's called on to assist. That's a given. But this one? This one's special. The more she watches the images from the cards, observes his behavior entering, standing under, and exiting the net, the stronger her feelings for him become. The way he moves through the world, tail held high while simultaneously eyeing his surroundings warily, strikes a chord of recognition in her. It's so much like the way she herself moves through the world, the same combination of caution and confidence that guides her along the pathways of her life's journey.

Solomon, she believes, is on his own journey. So far, its paths have been long, winding, and often convoluted. But they're *his* paths to follow, *his* journey to travel. Which is what makes this much more than a simple missing dog case to her. This particular dog is missing because he's chosen to be, over and over again. What does it mean? Why did he run? Why is he here, in Hull Village? It strikes her as such an odd choice, this place surrounded by water. Perhaps, one day, she'll know.

It takes a week and a half of preparing and setting out Solomon's food, scrolling through SD cards to observe his behavior at the net, and making note of how long it's taking him to eat. It feels like an eternity to Leslie, but finally the ARL is ready to drop the net.

On June 20, 2012, it's been nearly a year and a half since Solomon's odyssey through New England began. And as far as Alan's concerned, this is the day it's going to end. For good. The thing is, he doesn't know exactly what that end is going to look like. In the short term, they'll stick with the plan they'd established before the darting attempt: Solomon will be driven up to Maine and fostered by Hope. But then what? Will he ever be able to live in a home, as part of a family? He's clearly a flight risk, something he's proven several times over. Will he ever find a reason to stop running?

The thought of Solomon spending the rest of his life alone out-side—constantly on the run, and most likely with painful, debilitating, untreated heartworm and Lyme disease—doesn't sit well with Alan. This isn't what he gets up for every morning, isn't the reason he goes to work every day and often remains there well into the night. Is this what it's all going to come to in the end? A dog unable to live the kind of life dogs deserve to live? If so, the most humane thing for Solomon might be to put him down. But Alan's not ready to go there. Not yet.

And you never know, he thinks. Maybe the situation with Hope will turn out to be a foster fail. Lots of dogs find their home that way; why not Solomon? Happy ending, all around.

Alan, Brian, and Bill sit in the ARL van. Waiting, tense. One shot at this. That's all they're going to get. Three pairs of eyes dart and scan in every direction, hoping to get a few seconds' visual head start on Solomon's arrival. They have a clear view of the net and yard, are parked no more than a thirty-second dash away. We got this, Bill tells himself.

The plan, in theory, is simple. Wait until Solomon is under the center of the net, eating from the bowl with his head down. Hit the remote. Then leap out of the van and run like hell to the dropped net. Alan and Brian will step on the net's edges. Bill will put an additional hand-held net over Solomon as a secondary method of containment. If he's aggressive, Alan will have to dart him with the dart gun.

Assuming Solomon isn't aggressive, Alan will reach through the net, leash him, extricate him from the net, then put a slip lead on him. From there, over to the van and into the large crate waiting inside it. He'll be taken directly to the veterinary hospital, and once he's given a health clearance, Hope will drive down from Maine to pick him up. After that, there's no concrete, long-term plan. But no one's worried about the long-term at the moment; right now, their only concern is a successful drop and recovery.

Finally, Solomon appears at the net. They watch him trot across the yard, tail and ears up.

"There's our boy," Alan says. "Ready?"

"All set," Bill replies.

"Yup." Brian is ready. He's always ready, beyond prepared to do whatever it takes to bring an animal to safety. And yet, for a very brief moment, he experiences a twinge of regret on behalf of Solomon. The handsome dog confidently headed over to eat from under the net has no idea that, with one push of a remote button, life as he knows it will be over.

But like Alan, Brian believes the life Solomon has lived for the last year and a half is no life for a dog. Dogs belong with a family. By dropping the net on Solomon, they're ultimately helping him find that family. No reason to feel regret over that.

Solomon stands over a bowl of freshly cooked, soupy chicken. He's no longer cautious about going under the see-through object to eat. Whatever the object is doesn't touch him when he walks beneath it, and its open sides give him no reason to be wary. He stops briefly, ears up and alert, head turning left, then right. Making sure, as he always does, that he's alone. Reassured, he lowers his head and begins to eat, his tongue lapping the broth in little slurps.

"Here we go," Alan whispers.

They wait a few more seconds to make sure Solomon doesn't lift his head. The last thing they want is for him to look up and see the net dropping. Giving him any kind of a head start at getting out from under it would be like spotting Tom Brady a twenty-one-point lead before kickoff. The other team might as well go back to the locker room, get on their plane, and go home.

"Now!"

Solomon never hears the net before it drops on him; there's just the weight of something soft lying on his back, his head. There is no pain, just an odd heaviness surrounding his body, altering his vision. He shakes himself, managing only a slight, constricted sideways motion. He hears footsteps moving toward him, and voices. Panicked, he paws and tears at the net. And then, somehow, he finds an opening along the net's edge and squeezes through it. Free of the weight, he races to the safety of the hedges and trees, charges through the vegetation and out the other side, and keeps running.

The second Brian hits the remote, Alan and Bill leap from the van, followed immediately by Brian. But in the final yards separating them from the drop-net, Solomon manages to extricate himself from beneath it. They see a blur of black and white as Solomon tears off into the trees, and a net lying tangled, empty, on the ground.

For a moment, there are no words. And then the frustration of having somehow blown their one chance to net Solomon punctures the silence in bursts of profanity.

"Shit! Are you fucking kidding me?"

"Goddammit to hell! How the fuck did that happen?"

"I am so fucking *sick* of this," Bill shouts, slamming the pole net he's still holding to the ground. "Did the net malfunction, or what?"

Alan has no idea. Could the net have malfunctioned? Maybe. It had happened once before. Once, in all the years he's been doing this. But at this point, he's beginning to get the sense that it's not failed equipment that's making it impossible to recover this dog. It's something else entirely. Something kind of out there and weird. The sort of thing you can feel, but not understand.

But there are two things about the situation he understands just fine. Number one, Solomon is only the second dog in ARL history to escape from beneath a dropped net. And number two, he's gone.

Team Solomon is crushed by the failure of the drop-net. They worry that this latest fiasco may have finally pushed Solomon to the limit of his tolerance, set him on a path out of town.

And they worry about the dangers of summer. The year-round residents of Hull Village know to drive slowly in his neighborhood in case he unexpectedly runs across the street, spooked by something. But the tourists who visit the beaches don't know to do that, and neither do the summer residents. Increased summer home occupancy may mean the loss of some of Solomon's familiar, established hiding places, or changes to his daily routines. Then there's the Fourth of July; between the fireworks and the general chaos, it's the most stressful time of year for dogs on their own. And, most worrisome of all: the thriving, aggressive mosquito population in Hull Village. The likelihood of Solomon being re-infected with heartworm if he's out all summer is all but guaranteed.

If that happens, would he survive another winter on his own? No one wants to find out the hard way. The time to bring him to safety is now. But instead of Solomon being on his way to Maine with Hope, he's still on his own. Running.

Twelve

Beth sits on her couch, laptop open, clicking through the still shots Alan e-mailed of Solomon at and under the drop-net. The photos are date-stamped June 16 through June 20. The series shows Solomon traveling to and from the net, entering and exiting from all directions at random times of day. He's seemingly unconcerned about the existence of this latest oddity that's sprung up on his turf. In the background, Beth sees the edge of the porch he often naps beneath. Great set-up, she thinks. Kind of like rolling out of bed, walking a few feet to your kitchen, and discovering a delicious meal thoughtfully prepared and left there for you. Nice.

In every photo Solomon appears happy, confident. In one photo, he sits down under the net to scratch an itch behind his ear. In another he looks straight into the camera's lens and smiles.

"I am so in love with this dog," Beth confides to her own dogs Tamu and Poppy, stretched contentedly beside her. She wishes she could adopt Solomon herself. But after all that's happened since his arrival in Hull, she's beginning to believe his journey has a specific, pre-destined purpose. A purpose that includes her in exactly the role she's playing, and nothing more.

Reaching the end of the sequence of frames, she scrolls through them again. And again. She makes a video of the pictures, bringing the still shots to life. Mesmerized, she plays and re-plays the video. It's like a cartoon. The dog with the cow markings, who's somehow become larger than life, traveling in and out from under a big net. Eating, leaving, returning. Carefree. Until *swoosh*! The net falls on him, tangling him up in its clutches.

Ah, but wait! This is not the end of our hero. Like the Roadrunner, Superman, or Rocket J. Squirrel the dog prevails, escaping from the last best chance to nab him. As one of his would-be captors charges after him holding a dart gun resembling a bazooka, and another smashes his pole-net to the ground, the dog races away and out of sight.

"Yeah, kids would love this," Beth mutters. Solomon the Wonder Dog. It'd get great ratings, be the sleeper cartoon hit of the season. Too bad she's not an animator. When the ARL decided to set the drop-net she'd figured this was it, the beginning of the end of Solomon's travels. Never would she have predicted that Solomon would find a way to escape from under the net. Not with Alan and Brian in charge.

She goes back to the beginning of the video, plays it again to get to the part where the net drops. She sees Solomon on the ground beneath it, his body thrashing around and twisting under the weight of the net. Is he not tangled in it? He appears to be, but obviously not tangled to the point of being unable to free himself. Usually, the more a dog struggles to get out of the net the more tangled in it he becomes. But not Solomon.

It makes her think about something she read a while back on Wikipedia, about a man named Thomas Solomon. Born in 1969 in Milwaukee, Wisconsin, the escape artist and magician had extricated himself from just about every crazy place imaginable. An underwater bank safe made of titanium. Al Capone's prison cell. The irons that had shackled the legs of Billy the Kid. Lee Harvey Oswald's holding cell. And this was just a small sampling. The totality of his feats had earned him the "World's Greatest Escape Artist" award, bestowed by the Academy of Magical Arts and Sciences.

Beth wonders now if a name can become a self-fulfilling prophecy. If so, she figures that between the wisdom of King Solomon and Thomas

Solomon's talent for escape, Solomon the dog pretty much has things covered. So here they are again, thrown off balance either by recurring bad luck or Solomon's smarts, wondering what the outcome of this latest failure will be.

Will Solomon remain in Hull Village, or has the experience of a net dropping on him spooked him enough to make him move on? If he leaves Hull Village, where will he go? Relocation to another part of Hull would be the best-case scenario. But he might head out of Hull and into Hingham or Cohasset instead. Or pick up the rail tracks and end up pretty much anywhere. For all she knows, maybe he'll decide to swim across the bay over into Weymouth or Quincy. Beth puts absolutely nothing past Solomon at this point. The possibilities hurtling through her mind are endless.

She returns to the video, searching for possible clues to Solomon's state of mind. Although he bolts into the hedge, he doesn't seem to do so in a way that indicates irreparable trauma. She hopes she's reading it right. If she is, there's a good chance he's just laying low in one of his hiding places. If she's not, he's likely already on his way out of town, headed to parts unknown.

Late afternoon is settling in on the second day post drop-net when Beth's cell phone rings. She glances at the name on the screen: Leslie. Okay. This is either going to be very good or very bad. She's not ready to hear very bad, braces herself for the potential crash of it.

"Leslie…"

"He's still in Hull Village!"

Beth's body goes soft, her muscles and tendons releasing days' worth of tension.

"How do you know? Did you see him?"

"No. I just got a call from someone who saw him on the beach over by Jo's."

"Oh, thank goodness."

"I was afraid this might've been it, you know? The final straw from Solomon's perspective, the 'That's it, I'm outta here' moment."

"Yup. I thought the same thing. I think we all did."

Who knows why he's chosen to remain in Hull Village, Beth thinks. Could be that he's established a routine he's comfortable with, could be the ease of obtaining food and water. Or it could be something else altogether. But for whatever reason, they're apparently going to be given yet another chance to recover this elusive, majestic, aptly named dog.

Or are they? For the first time, Beth considers the possibility that Solomon doesn't want to be recovered. That he's content to live a solitary life in the tangential company of humans who provide for his basic survival needs. But it's only a fleeting consideration. Dogs are pack animals, and Beth has yet to meet a dog who prefers to live on his own. It's not that he doesn't want to live with people, she thinks. He just doesn't know how.

"So. Where do we go from here?" Beth asks.

"I have no clue. He won't go in the trap, the darting had to be called off, the drop-net failed. What's left?"

"The only thing we haven't tried is the Gypsy trap, the one we used at Covanta. I know it's a trap, but it's much larger than a standard trap and he may be less wary of it. And he did go into it once. Which may mean he'll go into again. It may also mean he'll never go into it again. No idea. Still, probably worth a try."

It sounds like a reasonable plan to Leslie. If he goes in, awesome. If he doesn't, which she considers much more likely, they're no worse off than before. Maybe by the time he's made it clear he's not going into this trap either, someone will have come up with a new idea.

"Okay, let's do it. How much space do we need to set it up? Do you have a place in mind?"

"So I'm thinking somewhere open, but kind of hidden from general viewing. That area next to Ella's playhouse would be perfect. Not in the grove, but on the other side of the playhouse, closer to Lisa's house. Do you think Lisa would agree to it? It does take up a good amount of space, but it's not dangerous."

"I'll ask her. I know she's concerned about Solomon and has gotten pretty attached to him, so I think she'll say yes."

They agree that if Lisa's okay with having the Gypsy trap in her yard, Beth will drive it down to Hull Village. If it's a no-go, the two of them will scout out another place together.

"He seems to have an unusually long memory for a dog," Beth muses. "I don't think we should risk introducing the trap too soon. It's only been two days since a net fell on him. And he also spent a lot of time around that trap. Wouldn't surprise me at all if he remembers it, and likely not in a good way."

"What do you think, then—a week? Two?"

"Let's say a week and a half."

"Okay. I'll talk with Lisa and we'll take it from there."

After the call with Beth, Leslie stretches out on her sofa. It's been an emotional, exhausting two days. Her last fully formed thought before falling dead asleep is that having a plan is good. Even if they have to wait another ten days to get it going.

Lisa walks across her yard carrying a plate of food and a quart jug of water, an empty bowl tucked under her arm. The original trap set for Solomon still sits in the grove just past Ella's playhouse, and this is once again where he's being fed. At least for now. She places the plate and bowl beside the trap, empties the water into the bowl, then goes back into the house to watch for him.

She's relieved he's still hanging around Hull Village. What is it, she wonders, about this neighborhood on a peninsula that not only drew him here, but keeps him here? Whatever it is, she believes it goes way beyond access to food, water, and shelter. He's capable of finding those things wherever he goes. It's odd, she knows, but there's something about him she finds transcendent, spiritual. Whatever it is he's seeking here, she believes it has much more to do with the soul than the body.

And perhaps that's why she feels so drawn to him, so centered when she sees him. It's as if the tumult in her mind, the fragmented pieces of her life, calm and become whole. She finds her heart and mind opening in unexpected ways. And she imagines what it would be like if Solomon were to join her family. She has no idea if he'll ever be able to live with people after having been on his own for so long. But in ten days, when Beth and Leslie set up the Gypsy trap, maybe she'll have the chance to find out.

Beth and Leslie lug the chain-link panels and steel poles of the Gypsy trap across Lisa's lawn. The panels are four feet wide and heavy, the late afternoon still warm, humid. They stop for a moment to rest their arm muscles.

"How'd you ever figure out how to make this thing?" Leslie asks, wiping the sweat from her face.

"Necessity, imagination. A lot of research. And an amazing electrical engineer."

They hoist the panels again, carrying them the rest of the way to the sheltered area by Ella's pink playhouse. As they work to get the trap set up, Beth slaps intermittently at her rear, legs, and arms. It's early July, the Hull Village mosquitos are out for blood, and hers is evidently particularly appetizing.

"*What* is with these mosquitos? They're biting my butt right through my pants."

They've intentionally not applied bug spray, worried the scent of it on the trap might repel not just mosquitos but Solomon.

"Yeah, the mosquitos down here suck. No pun intended. This is nothing. Wait'll later in the summer."

Beth very much hopes neither she nor Solomon will be in Hull Village later in the summer. A town with huge, aggressive mosquitos is absolutely *not* a place for a dog who's had heartworm to be hanging out. And, apparently, it's not a great place for her to be hanging out, either.

They work as speedily as they can to put the enclosure together. When it's all set up, they fit a chicken-wire covering over the top. Even though the panels are six feet high, it's not impossible for a trapped, frantic, intelligent dog to climb up and over them. The chicken wire should prevent that from happening, or at the very least buy them more time to get to the trap.

As an extra measure of security, Beth has augmented the enclosure with another panel. It provides four additional feet between the door and the trip line so that Solomon's deeper into the trap and farther from the door when the line trips.

"Okay, let me show you how this works," Beth says.

She opens the door to the enclosure and walks in, picking up a wire in the far right-hand corner.

"So this is the trip wire, and it's connected to this electromagnet right over here." She reaches out and connects the wire.

"Okay, so say you're Solomon. You smell the food … you walk into the enclosure—" She stops mid-sentence, looking expectantly at Leslie.

"What? Do you want me to actually do it?" Leslie asks.

"Yeah. That way you can see exactly how it works."

Leslie walks inside the Gypsy trap.

"So. Food over here, you're Solomon, you trot on over. On your way to the food you step on the trip wire, and voila! Door closes."

"Amazing." As the door closes smoothly behind her on its spring-loaded hinge, Leslie thinks the whole set-up is absolute genius. Standing inside feels nothing like what she'd always imagined being in a trap would feel like. It's roomy and unintimidating, and Solomon doesn't even have to go into the far end of it to reach the food. Experiencing the Gypsy trap firsthand, she sees why it worked at Covanta and why it might work again here in Lisa's yard.

The plan moving forward consists of three simple steps. Remove the standard trap and set the food outside the Gypsy trap for a week or two. Let Solomon get comfortable with it being there. Finally, when he starts acting like it's just another part of his landscape, move the food inside the trap and activate the trip wire.

In different circumstances, Beth would wait to activate the trip wire until a dog's behavior indicated a moderate level of comfort with entering the trap to eat. But this isn't just any dog. It's Solomon. They may get only one chance at this, so the trip wire will be live from the get-go.

Thirteen

Solomon jogs slowly along the beach below the Coast Guard station, the cool wet sand at the water's edge soothing to his paws, the late-day heat spreading uncomfortably through his body. His pace slows to a walk, then comes to a full stop. Panting, he stands for a moment, observing the water. The ripples along the shoreline are flat, almost non-existent, and he wades in without hesitation. He doesn't swim, needs to feel his paws in contact with solid ground. He walks in no deeper than his belly, and remains there until the welcome chill of cold water on his over-heated skin has spread to the rest of his body. Refreshed, he walks back to shore, shakes himself semi-dry. He bounds down the beach, then trots across the station's lawn and up the hill toward his shed.

Nearing his cut-through yard, Solomon smells food. He quickens his pace, following the scent across the yard. About halfway down the path leading to his shed, he finds the food placed beside something he knows wasn't there the last time he walked down the path. Still, there's something familiar in its shape. He has the sense he's encountered it before, and approaches with caution.

He sniffs at it, nose pressed against the metal, searching for clues. His unusually developed sense of smell and extraordinary scent recall detect two faint, familiar scents. He immediately turns his head, looking for the humans he knows to be their source. These humans often appear where he is, but his eyes and nose confirm they're not there now.

He identifies other scents on the object. Some are vaguely familiar and human, the rest unfamiliar and canine. He takes his time walking the perimeter of the object, stopping every so often to stare at it, to thoroughly smell each panel.

Suddenly, he stops sniffing. He pulls back from the panel, tilts his head to one side. He approaches again, face up against the metal bars, and breathes in deeply. The hairs rise along his spine. There is no mistaking the scent, even diluted by time. It's the smell of fear, and he recognizes it as his own. He backs away, ears flat against his head. He will eat the food beside this oversized box. But he will not go inside it again.

By now, Beth figures, she could make the drive from Newton to Hull Village with her eyes closed. She and Leslie are parked across the street from Lisa's house, the sight line to the activated Gypsy trap perfect, unobstructed. They've spent long hours, alone and together, staking out. Tried every kind and combination of human food to lure Solomon into the trap. And still it continues. Mid-July and counting.

The thing that really gets them? Solomon almost always trots by their stake-out car on his way to somewhere else, shooting them a look as he passes. Cool as a cuke, Beth thinks. Throwing shade.

"Here he comes," Leslie observes.

"And there he goes," Beth replies. "He's probably thinking 'Hey-hey, ladies. Nice to see you again. Sorry I can't hang around, but I'm dining out this evening.'"

"And then he probably laughs his ass off," Leslie says.

As the days pass and Solomon resolutely refuses to enter the Gypsy trap, he's regularly seen over at Jo's. Customers toss leftover fried clams and burgers off the deck for him, and sometimes people see him eating crabs or fish washed ashore. Leslie reports these continued sightings to Beth.

"The tough thing is, he doesn't need us for food," Leslie says as they chat on the phone about Solomon. "He's perfectly capable of finding his own, or getting people besides us to provide it for him."

"Highly resourceful, that dog. You know, I've been thinking we may want to try a different kind of food. We recovered a dog up on the North Shore a while ago with Tripett."

"What's Tripett?"

"It's a dog food made from green beef tripe, tripe that still has partially digested food in it. It's absolutely disgusting. Seriously, the smell of it makes you want to vomit. But dogs love it."

At this point, they agree, anything's worth a try. The worst that can happen is that whoever baits the trap gets sick, and Solomon ignores the Tripett. Remove the potential vomiting from the equation, and the scenario's basically status quo. What do they have to lose?

"I have a pretty strong stomach," Leslie says. "I'm happy to pick the stuff up and set it in the trap."

"Okay. Let me know when you have it, and I'll drive down to stake out with you."

Leslie's search for Tripett has taken on an epic quality. Like the search for the Holy Grail, or the quest to trap Solomon. She walks out to her car from her third useless trip into a pet supplies store, feeling frustrated but determined.

"Oh, I'm going to find this Tripett," she tells herself. "And when I do? I'm going to buy a freakin' case of it."

Back in her car, Leslie Googles 'who makes Tripett dog food.' Turns out it's a brand called PetKind. She Googles 'who carries PetKind,' then enters her zip code. A map with a scattering of red pins appears, and she scans it for the pin closest to Hull.

When she sees the name of the town that red pin is located in, Leslie laughs at the irony of it. This has to be the Universe's idea of a joke, she thinks. Because the nearest place to buy Tripett is an aquarium and pet supply store in Canton. The last town Solomon was seen in before he turned up nearly three weeks later in Hull. The red pin is like a visual ha-ha, a reminder of their lack of progress toward recovering Solomon. Touché, Universe, she thinks. Touché.

She doesn't have time to drive to Canton now, but she'll call the store to make sure they have Tripett in stock before heading over tomorrow. She suspects it's not a best-seller, and may not be frequently ordered by the store. Still, she figures there are probably at least a few cans in stock, if not the case she wants to buy. Hopefully, a can or two will be all they'll need.

Beth and Leslie are in the ACO van, parked on the street in front of Lisa's house. The stale air inside the van is sticky and still. Leslie reaches into the backpack on the floor by her feet, rummages around in it until she finds a hair clip. She grabs her long, sweat-damp hair at the nape, twists it around a few times, then clips it high up off her neck. Much better.

A plate stacked high with what both women believe to be the most vile-smelling dog food on the planet awaits Solomon inside the Gypsy trap. Now, he just needs to pass by close enough to catch the scent of the new food they hope will lure him into the trap. If they're lucky, this will be it.

Inside, Lisa stations herself in front of the window with the best view of the Gypsy trap. She says a silent prayer, hoping her positive thoughts and energy will guide Solomon into the trap. He's so close to the end of his literally unbelievable journey, so close to having another chance at a happy life. Still, if Solomon is finally recovered today, her heart will break more than a little. She's given up on the idea of Solomon living with her family, convinced herself he'll be better off living in Maine with Hope.

Her life is too upended right now, too chaotic. And she knows nothing about dogs. She's a cat person. Why had she ever imagined Solomon could become a part of her family? Certain there's a better family than her own out there for him, she closes her eyes and visualizes Solomon walking into the Gypsy trap, the door closing securely behind him, Beth and Leslie moving toward him, leashes in hand. May it all be so.

They've been waiting for over an hour. What if he just plain refuses to enter the trap, even for Tripett? What will they do next? Each pushes the thought from her mind, concentrates instead on creating positive vibes. Perhaps their efforts are successful, because suddenly they see Solomon approaching the trap, materializing as if out of nowhere.

"I don't know why, but I thought he'd walk past us, not come up the path from the back. He must've been napping in his shed," Leslie says. From what she's been able to piece together over the last few months regarding Solomon's behavior and routine, this is a little out of the ordinary. He's usually out and about at this hour, not napping. She hopes he's okay.

"Maybe the smell of the Tripett woke him up. Wouldn't surprise me."

They watch as he moves toward the Gypsy trap, tail wagging in anticipation of locating and devouring this new and particularly aromatic meal. But when he sees the food is inside the structure, Solomon halts abruptly. He stands very still, staring fixedly at the chain-link panels, head slightly cocked.

"Yup. He definitely remembers he was trapped in that thing once," Beth says.

Leslie is sure Beth's right. Solomon's too smart to not recognize the Gypsy trap. Still, he appears curious, resumes his approach. He walks slowly around the trap, sniffing, observing the hinges.

"Look at him, Beth. He's doing the same thing he did with the first trap, trying to figure out how it works, trying to see if there's a way he can eat the food without getting trapped."

"I know. There's not, though. Once that wire's tripped, the door closes super fast."

"Do you think he might see the trip wire and step over it?"

The thought has never occurred to Beth. Until now.

"That's probably giving him too much credit. I'm not sure any dog, even Solomon, is that smart." Still, she pushes the thought away. Better not to imagine or dwell on those kinds of things. Especially when it comes to Solomon.

Leslie finds Beth's opinion reassuring. If Solomon will just go into the trap, that'll be it. Done. Finished. Over and out. Still, Solomon continues his assessment of the Gypsy trap, seemingly weighing his options. The purposeful way he circles the trap—scrutinizing, sniffing, digging at the ground beneath the panel closest to the Tripett—sets Leslie on edge again. What if he really *can* figure it out, really does see and avoid the trip wire? Stop it, she orders herself silently. Seriously. Don't even go there.

As three pairs of eyes follow his every movement, Solomon appears to conclude he can't dig the food out of the trap. If he wants it, he's going to have to go into the enclosure to get it. He abandons his digging and walks around to the entrance of the Gypsy trap. Inside the van, the silence of held breath is counterpointed by the whine of cicadas and fragments of summer birdsongs.

Solomon pokes his head across the plane of the trap's open door and stands there, as if waiting to see what will happen. When nothing does, he walks just inside and once again stands still, waiting. He's right in front of the opening, able to easily and immediately exit should anything spook him. But all seems unthreatening, and he moves toward the food.

"Here we go. Get ready!" Beth murmurs.

Leslie can't believe they're almost there, that Solomon's unlikely journey is nearly over. Just a few more steps and they'll have him. She's already looking forward to following what she hopes will be his very happy life. As Solomon takes those last few steps toward the plate of Tripett, Leslie listens for the slam of the Gypsy trap's door.

But she never hears it. It's her eyes that clue her in to what's gone down; her eyes that refuse to look away from the sight of Solomon wolfing down Tripett, the door to the trap standing part-way open. Somehow, the door has failed to close completely, leaving an opening large enough for Solomon to squeeze through. As unbelievable as it is, the unthinkable has happened once again.

From the window, Lisa watches as Solomon enters the Gypsy trap. This is it, she tells herself, her heart beating so hard she's surprised Solomon can't hear it all the way across the yard. Her constant worrying is about to come to an end. No more wondering if he's too hot, or too hungry, or too lonely. No more concern about him being wet and shivering from the rain, or feasted on by mosquitos and ticks. He's actually, finally, *in the trap*. The door is going to shut any second now, and he'll be safe.

But as she watches Solomon approach the plate of food she begins to panic. From where she sits she can see the trap's door ajar. Or at least it looks that way to her. Maybe it's just the angle, or a shadow. Still, if the door is closed and Solomon's trapped, why haven't Beth and Leslie arrived at the trap by now? The plan is to get there right away, in case Solomon figures out a way to escape. What are they doing? What's taking so long?

Lisa peers anxiously out the window at the trap, questions churning in her mind, until she sees Solomon approach the door. She watches him squeeze his large, well-fed body through the opening. Then she sees him turn and stare at the door. She's sure he recognizes that the space is much narrower now than when he entered through it. He looks across the yard at the van, then trots briskly down the path toward his shed. Clearly, the opening she thought she'd seen from the window wasn't an angle or a shadow. Somehow the trap has malfunctioned.

Lisa grabs onto the windowsill for support, takes a few deep, conscious breaths, and then a few more. She does this until the exhale is more smooth than fluttering, until the odd tingling of her scalp disappears. Her vision of what would happen after Solomon entered the trap is still so vivid, so hard to release from her mind and heart. In that vision, she waits until Solomon is safely in the Gypsy trap. There's a leash attached to his dirty, weathered collar, and a slip lead around his neck for extra security. She joins Beth and Leslie inside the trap and reaches out to touch Solomon gently. A touch to let him know he's been cared about, that his presence in her life has mattered. A touch to say good-bye.

None of that's going to happen now. It makes her heart ache to acknowledge it, but she knows he'll never go in the trap again. She rarely thinks like this, is usually wide open to serendipity and possibility. But after seeing the way he looked at the door after squeezing through it, she knows they've just had their one and only chance with the Gypsy trap. And that somehow, that chance got away.

One of her cats comes over to brush up against her leg, to comfort with a head butt. She picks him up, buries her face in the sweet smell of his fur.

"Solomon was right there," she tells the cat. "We had him. And now we don't."

"I can't believe it," Beth says. "Really. I just can't."

Leslie rolls down the window and leans her head out, the fresh air an antidote to her nausea.

"How did that happen?" she asks.

"No idea. The battery could've chosen the worst time possible to die. There could be a little ridge on the ground, or a rock, or twig, or something else we didn't see when we set the thing up. Or the Universe could just be getting off on screwing with us again."

It really does seem to Leslie that some invisible *something* is out to get them, laughing at their attempts to recover this dog. But from her perspective, it's not funny. Solomon had to have noticed that the trap's door was in a different position when he exited than when he entered.

How could he not? He had to squeeze through a space on the way out that he easily passed through on the way in. He knows he could've been trapped, won't repeat his mistake.

"He's never going in there again, is he."

Beth prefers to avoid absolutes.

"It's doubtful. But he did go in and get himself back out, so if he's hungry enough and there's sufficiently appetizing food, he might venture back in. You can never say 'never' with these things. But I'd probably give it no more than a one percent chance. Maybe two."

One percent, maybe two. Well, Leslie thinks, those odds certainly suck, but a one-to-two-percent chance is an improvement over never. The situation is what it is. There's nothing they can do about it except try to figure out why the door malfunctioned.

"Want to go check out the trap, see what happened with the door?" she asks Beth.

"Might as well."

They walk to the Gypsy trap in silence, then squeeze sideways through the same small space Solomon passed through no more than five minutes ago. Examining the ground closely, they search for small rocks or sticks that might have caused the door to jam.

"I don't see anything. Do you?" Leslie asks.

"No. And the ground right here is level, so the door should've just swung shut. It must be the battery. I'll take it home to charge it. In the meantime, let's leave the trap open without making it live for a while. Just to see if he'll go in again."

It's not the best plan they've ever come up with, Leslie thinks. But it's the only one they've got.

Down the path and over the wall from Ella's playhouse, Solomon lies in his shed. He is awake, alert. His ears point upward, catching the sounds of the two voices coming from the place he just left. If the sounds get closer he's ready to spring up, hop over the window sill, and relocate to a safer hiding place. The voices are, by now, familiar to him, and he usually experiences them as neutral. But their current tone is different, sharper. He remains vigilant, body taut, ready to bolt. He listens until the voices fade and disappear. Then he listens for a while after that, listens until he knows the humans are gone. Eventually his breathing slows, his ears relax. With his stomach full, he falls into a heavy sleep.

Beth carries the Gypsy trap's marine battery into the house and sets it down in the living room. Her dogs greet her, whining to be let out. She opens the door and watches them race into the yard to do their business, then heads into the kitchen for something to drink. For a moment she considers pouring herself a stiff one. But drinking adult beverages in the heat always seems to make everything about a hot, lousy day even hotter, more miserable. She sighs. Iced tea it is.

As she watches the tea bags float, then sink under the weight of her spoon before cheerfully popping back up again, the events of the day replay themselves in her mind. The image of Solomon walking through the almost-closed door of the trap into the freedom of Lisa's yard will never be erased from her memory. And maybe that's a good thing in the end, she thinks. More fuel for the fire, more motivation to prevail.

Iced tea made and poured, Beth walks back to the living room. She sees the dogs through the screen door, sitting patiently on the step, waiting to be let in.

"Okay guys, c'mon in, settle down. Want to take a look at this battery with me? Help me charge it up, figure out what's wrong with it?"

She laughs as both dogs turn, head for their beds. "Didn't think so."

Once the charger is connected to the battery, she peers at the indicator in disbelief. The battery is about three-quarters charged.

"What the hell?" she asks aloud, staring at the battery. "How can this thing be seventy-five percent charged?" It makes no sense. If the battery was charged to that level, there's no way it wouldn't have had sufficient juice to work the trap. So why hadn't the door closed?

She's a logical person. But over the past two months she's slowly, grudgingly, come to believe there's an unseen force working against Solomon's recovery. Working overtime, in fact. What she doesn't understand is why. Why is the goal of bringing this amazing dog to safety and giving him the chance to have a normal dog life with a loving family so wrong, so offensive?

Beth ponders it all for a very long time. She replays the video of Solomon escaping from the drop-net, thinks back to the darting day when things had gone all kinds of wrong. She goes back even further: his break out from the D'Arpinos' yard, his misery at the ARL, his escape from Carmen and Steve in Kittery. The only place he's been happy, it seems, was at Covanta—and then they'd trapped him. And now, he appears perfectly content to be in Hull Village, once again living on his own with some help from his friends.

So is that what it's all about? Is Solomon truly meant to exist as a lone dog, a pack animal without a pack, living around people but not with them? Perhaps. Still, she has the feeling it's more complicated than that. Maybe it's not even about him living on his own. Maybe it's really about him choosing where he lives and who he lives with, instead of having others decide those things for him.

Or, to delve even deeper into the existential, maybe it's about Solomon's destiny. He's come all this way to fulfill it, refusing to remain where he wasn't meant to be, always moving forward, searching for the place he belongs. But will he know that place when he finds it? And is it in Hull Village? She has no idea. But she wonders if their good intentions are interfering with Solomon's ability to find his home, his people. Maybe it really is time for all of them to butt out and let whatever it is that guides him lead him home.

Fourteen

Lisa sits at the kitchen island, blowing on her too-hot cup of tea, thinking about Solomon. She reflects, not for the first time, on the many attempts to recover him, the odd and unpredictable ways in which each has failed. Maybe, she thinks, it's just not his destiny to be caught. Maybe he's meant to come inside on his own timetable, with dignity. The more she thinks about it all, the more strongly she believes it really may be as simple as that.

And she believes something else, too: that he's meant to choose where he lives, to choose his family. The journey that's brought him here, whether destiny or something not nearly that spiritually heavy, is his own path to walk. The many well-intentioned efforts to recover Solomon have failed because their success would create roadblocks and detours on that path.

She's sure Solomon knows he's being hunted. How could he not? Yet he's still here. Despite the darting attempt, despite the drop net, despite what she's convinced he knows was a narrow escape from a trap, he stays. For some reason, his drive to remain in Hull Village is stronger than a dog's natural instinct to flee a place where he's become prey. That has to mean *something*.

Like everyone else, Lisa wants Solomon to be safe. Even so, she's beginning to feel she can no longer support efforts to trap him and bring him back to Maine. Or even to trap him at all. It feels to her, now, an affront to Solomon's spirit to catch him by tangling him in a net, or shooting him with a dart, or corralling him in a trap. There has to be a better way to help him to the safe end of his travels, to the ending he chooses for himself. She intends to do everything she can to figure out what that better way might be.

With the exception of Lisa, no one is ready to give up on the Gypsy trap. She considers asking Beth and Leslie to remove it from her property, but decides against it. She's convinced Solomon won't go in it unaware of the likelihood of being trapped. Which means he probably won't go in it at all.

So as July melts into August and August into September, Lisa and Leslie continue placing Solomon's food in the non-activated Gypsy trap. To no one's surprise, Solomon never sets foot inside the trap again. He has no way of knowing it's not live. What he does know is that he was almost trapped inside the last time he entered it. He won't take that risk again, is finding his food elsewhere.

"I don't think there's any point in continuing to set food in the trap," Leslie tells Lisa one day in early September.

"I don't, either. Maybe just leave his food outside the trap?" It bothers Lisa that Solomon has been seen making his rounds again. That he's scavenging meals of cast-off food when he could be eating good, healthy meals prepared just for him—if it wasn't left inside a trap he has no intention of entering.

"Makes sense to me. Let me run it by Beth, though. Just to be sure."

Leslie's call to Beth goes straight to voice mail.

"Hey, Beth, it's Leslie. Give me a call when you can. Thanks."

It's early evening when Beth calls. "Leslieee! What's up?"

"Oh, you know. Cat up a tree, off-leash dog crapping in a neighbor's yard, bat flying around in someone's house. The usual. You?"

"Everything's good. Busy, but good. And, still thinking about our boy Solomon, trying to figure out a new plan."

"That's why I called. Lisa and I have been leaving food in the trap for about six weeks. At this point, I'm a hundred percent sure he's never going in there again. But now, instead of hanging out at Lisa's and eating there, he's back to traveling his routes, eating who knows what. I'm thinking it'd make more sense to leave the food outside the trap, keep him close, and work on figuring out what to do next. What do you think?"

"Yup. Absolutely what we want. We're lucky to have a cooperative home owner; let's take advantage of it."

"Okay, sounds good."

"Thanks, Leslie. You're putting in the lion's share of work on this case. Much appreciated."

"I'm honored to be part of Team Solomon. Really. Talk soon."

Solomon moves stealthily through the marshes, looking for a rodent or perhaps a gull to ease the tight pain in his belly. The marsh grass, still high, nicks his legs, the summer sharpness of the blades like tiny razors. But on this late morning his hunting is unsuccessful. He pushes his way through and out of the marsh, crosses the street, and heads toward Jo's Nautical Bar.

As he trots along the short beach in front of Jo's the late summer sun warms his back, reflecting off his coat, making him shine. The smells from this place always draw him, and he never leaves hungry. Looking up at the deck he sees no one. He walks down to the water and wades in. The dead crabs, fish, and occasional sea bird all end up right along the shoreline, and ankle-deep is as far in as he ever needs to go.

Finding nothing edible along the water's edge, he plops down on the sand in the sun. Something in the salt air, though, stirs his senses, awakens the urge to play. He spots a few small white creatures moving along the sand farther down by the water. Leaping up, he chases after them. They scatter wildly at his approach, squawking and flapping, then rise into the air above him, out of reach.

He's disappointed, but only briefly. The white creatures return to the sand, just a few feet from where they'd lifted away, and he races after them. Again they disappear from the sand, again they return. He barks and prances happily around them, lowering his belly to the sand, the tail end of his body in the air. He repeats these actions over and over again until, spent of energy, he heads up to his favorite napping place under Jo's deck. He falls asleep almost immediately.

A short time later, he's jolted awake by the sound of shuffling and scraping above him. Solomon gets up and stretches, then emerges onto the beach from the cool shade below the deck. He squints, eyes adjusting to the sunlight, and sits on the warm sand in view of the people on the deck. He remains there, waiting patiently, until bits of burgers and fries, hot dogs and fish begin to fly off the deck. They're his for the taking, and he gulps them down.

He usually stays until the ache in his belly disappears. But the salty food has made him thirsty, and he trots off down the sand. At the end of the beach he heads toward a house he's discovered on his travels. The house has a shady yard and a small source of fresh water, set at the perfect height for him to drink from. Today there are tiny creatures perched on the edge of the water. They chirp angrily at his approach, but Solomon is undeterred, focused on the water he needs. The creatures, still scolding, scatter into the trees. And then he has the cool, clean water to himself.

Refreshed, Solomon ambles back along the beach, then up the hill toward his cut-through yard. As soon as he steps from the street into the yard, he smells the food. A few steps farther, and he sees the plate set beside the metal structure, near the path to his shed. He makes a beeline for the food, then stands over it. For a moment he watches, listens; then he drops his head and devours the food, licking the plate perfectly clean.

Lisa looks out the window, observing Solomon as he eats the meal she's set out for him. Backlit by the sun he looks incandescent. Every day since she began feeding him outside the Gypsy trap again, she's moved his food a bit farther from the trap, closer to the house. She's sure he notices the small incremental changes in location, but they don't seem to bother him.

And Solomon isn't the only one who notices the traveling plate.

"How come you moved Solomon's food, Mommy?" Ella asks one morning.

"Because I want to see him better. Don't you?"

Ella nods. "I love Solomon."

"Me, too."

But there's more to it than that. Seeing him, knowing he's survived another night to appear for breakfast, that he's successfully navigated his way through another day to return for dinner, is affirming, uplifting. In his unrelenting quest to find whatever it is he's searching for he's become a touchstone for her, a centering force she needs to be in the presence of.

Lisa allows herself to once again imagine Solomon joining her family, to entertain the possibility that her big, sunny house is where he's meant to be. She has no way of knowing if her imaginings are rooted in even the slightest truth. But wouldn't it be amazing if they were. If the reason he's stayed in Hull Village all this time is because he's been waiting for her to realize why he's there.

She feels an overwhelming need to talk to him, to connect in the only way she's able. And so she continues to move his food, until one day he's just barely close enough to hear her.

If she'd thought too much about it she might not have done it, might've decided it wasn't worth the risk. Months earlier, Beth and

Leslie had shared two of the cardinal rules of engagement when trying to recover a dog: "Don't look the dog in the eyes, and don't speak to him." Dogs living on their own can experience these actions as aggression and may run, panicked. Still, a small inner voice overrides reason, instructs her otherwise. Talk to him, it urges her. Just do it. It's what he needs. It'll be alright.

And so she does, beginning what will become twice daily monologues. She speaks softly, her tone low and steady. But she knows he can hear her, observes him lift his head from the plate, tilt his head in the direction of her voice, ears raised.

"Hi, Solomon. I hope you had a good night, and that you were comfortable in your shed or under your porch. And I hope you like your breakfast. It's got all kinds of good stuff in it. You're such a good boy, so smart. You probably don't know it, but everyone around here thinks you're pretty special. I hope your day is happy and safe, and brings you closer to whatever it is your heart's looking for."

Solomon stands, ears up and turned outward, head cocked in the direction of the voice. It's a voice he recognizes. Sometimes, he catches bits of it drifting through the window of his shed. Other times, he hears it when he's cutting through the yard. This is the first time, though, that he's heard the voice while he eats. It's low and soft, devoid of threat. He experiences the tone of it as soothing.

Though he understands nothing of what is being communicated through the sounds, there's something about their inflections that makes him want to stay, to listen. It never occurs to him to run, as he has so often from similar sounds. Instead, he remains grounded to his spot in front of the plate of food, listening. The sounds stop abruptly, and he waits for them to resume. When they don't, he lowers his head and eats the breakfast that's been prepared for him with chicken, ham, eggs, hope, and love.

PART THREE

Finding
Home

Fifteen

Hull Village, Massachusetts: October/November 2012

Solomon snaps awake. A loud, whistling, shrieking noise rattles and shakes the walls of his shed. He shivers in the damp cold, curls deeper into himself. The noise continues. Unable to sleep, he lies on the rain-soaked floor of the shed, listening to the sounds outside, processing their clues. Is he safe, or should he run? He needs to go outside, doesn't want to soil his sleeping space. But he represses those needs for as long as he can, until he's certain the sounds outside pose no danger.

Rising from his curled position on the floor he stretches backward, forward, then shakes himself. He moves to the window and looks through it. Clouds of brown leaves swirl ferociously, and the rain falls in sideways sheets. The wildness of it excites him. He jumps gracefully over the windowsill and out into the elements. Halfway down the drive-way he relieves himself against a tree. Then, gait tilted sideways into the wind, he walks to the end of the driveway and turns left toward the booming ocean.

Outside the clattering walls of the shed, Solomon experiences a sense of exhilaration. The turbulent winds, gusting hard off the water, awaken something primitive within him. He instinctively knows not to walk along the water's edge. Instead, he travels the side of the road farthest from the ocean. Still, an occasional freezing wetness splashes his body as waves crash forcefully against the seawall, spraying foam and water up over the wall and across the street. He hasn't felt this kind of pure happiness in a very long time.

Eventually he tires of walking. Pushing against the strength of the wind has exhausted him, and he heads back in the direction of his shed. The return walk, with the wind at his back, is easier, and as his energy returns so does his joyfulness. Alone outside in the storm, he sees no one to avoid, to run from. None of the moving objects he normally watches for in the street, is careful not to walk in front of. The world, right now, is his alone.

Solomon steps off the sidewalk and into the empty road. He sits in the middle of it, then lifts his head, nose pointed upward, inhaling the salt air. His senses absorb it all—the noise, the wetness, the smell, the raging wildness. He lets out a series of barks that even those unfamiliar with the language of dogs would understand to be joy. And when his barking ceases still he sits, the canine eye of a glorious storm.

Everyone on Team Solomon is in a state of high anxiety. It's October 29, 2012, and Hurricane Sandy is barreling up the Massachusetts coast. The storm's sustained winds measure 70 miles per hour, with gusts of 85 miles per hour. For anyone living near the ocean, it's a dangerous day to be outside. But it's particularly dangerous for a dog on his own.

Will Solomon know he should stay sheltered, even if it means he won't eat, or will hunger drive him out into the storm? What if he heads down to the beach and gets swept away by the waves? What if he's hit by a tree branch, or steps on a downed power line? The possibilities are endless. Horrifying. The more Leslie turns each one over in her mind the more her dread grows. She calls Beth, hoping Beth can talk her off the ledge.

"Do you think he'll stay put?" Leslie asks.

"I hope so." Beth also hopes the noise and wind from the storm won't have a fireworks effect, making him bolt from wherever he's sheltering. No point in sharing that thought with Leslie, though. Totally unhelpful.

"All those times we almost had him, and now this. If anything happens to him, I don't think I'll ever get over it."

Beth knows exactly what Leslie means.

"I think he's going to be okay, Leslie. We all know how smart he is. His instincts will keep him inside and safe."

Their conversation is interrupted by another call coming in on Leslie's phone.

"Call you back in a few," she tells Beth, then takes the call.

🐕

"Is this the Hull Animal Control Officer?" the man asks.

"Yes, this is Leslie Badger."

"So I just want to let you know that I was out walking around, checking out the wave action?"

Is this guy serious? Who in their right mind would consider that a good judgement call?

"Okay…"

"And that big black and white dog everybody's been trying to catch all summer? He was sitting right in the middle of the road, in all that rain and wind! Just thought I should let you know."

For a moment, Leslie is too shocked to speak. Could Solomon really be out walking around in the middle of a hurricane? If so, he's behaving contrary to all assumptions and expectations. Again.

"Where exactly did you see the dog?"

"Not too far up past the Coast Guard station."

Based on the location, it has to be him. Holy shit. What was he doing out there in the middle of the road? No one's ever seen him do anything like that. Not to her knowledge. This is a dog who looks both ways before crossing the street, not one who sits in the middle of it. Unless—

"Did he look like he was hurt?"

"Not that I could see. Can't say for sure that he wasn't, though."

"Okay, I'll go check it out. Thanks for the call. And do me a favor, okay? Stay inside. There's a hurricane out there."

Leslie heads out to the ACO van in her foul weather gear but doesn't get far. One look at the water in the street and she knows she's not driving anywhere.

Besides, what will she do if she sees Solomon? It's not like he's going to hop in the van if she opens the door for him. That's only her most frequent, most cherished daydream. It's not going to happen in real life. Even if he's injured, he'll try to run. Unless he's lying in the road unable to move, she's not going to be able to recover him. She goes back inside and calls Beth, relays the information from the caller.

"So now we know Solomon's out walking around in a hurricane. Unbelievable."

Beth has to admit it. Solomon's behavior is, truly, unbelievable.

"Yup. Definitely doing nothing I thought he'd do. But then again, does he ever?"

Leslie laughs, mostly because it seems like the only appropriate response to the frustrating truth of Beth's comment.

"So. Let's remember how smart Solomon is. I really think his smarts will keep him safe," Beth says.

Leslie agrees; Solomon is probably the smartest dog ever. Possibly even smarter than some people. She wonders if there's a way to test a dog's IQ. If there is, she'll pay to have Solomon's tested when this is over. Still, she can't shake the image of Solomon in the middle of the street, or what it might mean, from her mind.

"I know, you're right. But don't you think it's weird that he'd be sitting in the road like that? My biggest fear is that he's hurt. I'm going to call Lisa and ask her to keep an eye out for him."

"He could be hurt. But he could also be sitting in the middle of the road, in the middle of a hurricane, just for the fun of it, you know? Just because he's Solomon."

"Yeah, I guess so." This *is* Solomon they're talking about. Anything's possible. There's no figuring him out.

"Hopefully, when this has all blown out to sea tomorrow, or north, or wherever it's heading next, he'll pop up in Lisa's yard looking for his breakfast, not a scratch on him."

That's the image Leslie intends to hold onto. Solomon the Teflon dog; scratch-resistant, water resistant. It'll all turn out fine.

"I'll let you know if I get any more calls about him today. Otherwise, let's plan to talk tomorrow."

"Sounds good. Stay safe, Leslie."

"You, too. Talk soon."

The wind rattles the windows in the yellow Victorian. Lisa wonders if she should have followed her neighbors' lead and taped them. She reminds herself that the old house has been through worse coastal storms and survived. It'll survive this one, too. She's much more concerned for the folks who live right along the water. But her greatest concern is for Solomon.

Where is he? What is he doing? She hopes he's under the porch of the big white house. That's where she thinks he'll be safest. She worries that if he's in the shed, the glass remaining in its window might implode on him. Or that the shed itself might collapse in a gust of hurricane-force wind, burying him beneath its debris.

Lisa forces those images from her mind. She breathes deeply, visualizes Solomon tucked into the far reaches of the space beneath the porch. In her vision, his back is secure against the foundation wall, his body curled up tightly. He is warm, unafraid. Almost as soon as she conjures this image of Solomon, though, her thoughts begin to wander.

His stomach is probably rumbling by now; it's way past time for his breakfast. According to the meteorologists, Sandy will pass quickly over Massachusetts and tomorrow will be a better day. She'll put something extra-special out for him tomorrow morning, first thing. But what about today, when he's hungry?

Lisa acknowledges the thoughts. Then she pushes them gently away, continues her deep breathing and visualization. He is safe under his porch, tomorrow will bring a calming of wind and rain, he will be fine. And then Leslie calls, and Lisa is back at her windows, heart in her throat, watching for a possibly injured Solomon.

By the next day Sandy has moved on. Hull's streets are waterlogged, strewn with sand and rocks. Broken tree limbs litter neighborhood yards and sidewalks. Power lines are down in some areas of town. Still, the destruction pales in comparison to the images of devastation Lisa sees on the Boston news stations. The coastal areas of New York and New Jersey are nearly unrecognizable, and Lisa knows the Massachusetts coast dodged a bullet with this one. But had Solomon done the same?

Standing in front of the stove scrambling some eggs, Lisa distractedly pushes the eggs around the frying pan with the spatula. Leslie's phone call from the day before plays over and over in her mind. It's difficult to rein in her imagination, to not focus on all the terrible things that could've happened to Solomon during and after the storm. She concentrates on Solomon safe under his porch, or wherever he's found shelter. He wakes, goes outside, and heads toward her house in search of breakfast. If she sees these images clearly enough, maybe they'll come true.

The eggs are done. Overdone, really, but Solomon won't care. Especially when they're mixed in with the ham she's prepared for him. After not eating yesterday he'll be hungry, and a delicious, protein-rich breakfast is just what he needs. Lisa carries the plate of food down the steps of the back porch into the yard. She places the food two feet closer to the house than it had been two days earlier. Back inside, she pulls a chair from the dining room table over to one of the windows overlooking the backyard. She settles down in the chair with her coffee, stares out the window into the yard, and waits.

It's not long before Solomon appears. Drawn by the aroma of freshly cooked food, he hurries across the yard from the area by Ella's playhouse.

That means he probably spent the night in his shed, Lisa figures, with the wind and rain blowing in through the barely-there windows and the big gap in the doorway.

Her heart beats faster at the sight of him. His gait looks perfectly normal, and his head and tail are up. He's weathered the storm just fine. Still. The thought of him spending more than a full day cold and wet bothers her deeply. Today, she decides, is the day she will do something about the situation.

In the meantime, she watches Solomon wolf down his food. She doesn't open the window to talk to him, worries he may have residual trauma from yesterday's events. Outwardly, though, he seems perfectly relaxed and happy. Maybe he took the whole thing in stride, just another day in the neighborhood. She'll never know. What she does know is that he's alive and well, eating from a china plate in her backyard. And that, she thinks, is everything.

Lisa has no idea if Solomon's ever had his own toys. But by the time she's through shopping at PetSmart this morning, he'll have a whole pile of toys. Just thinking about it makes her smile. She yanks a small plastic shopping basket with handles out of a stack of identical baskets and heads off to the dog toys section. If she'd been open to selecting any type of dog toy, she might've been at PetSmart for hours, overwhelmed by the selection. Balls of all kinds. Various sizes and colors of an oddly shaped, hard rubber chew toy called a Kong. Tug toys, puzzle toys, toys for playing fetch, and toys that make a crinkle sound. Toys with stuffing, toys without.

Lisa, though, is looking for a specific kind of toy. Something fuzzy that Solomon can curl up with for comfort and warmth. Further down the aisle, she hits the jackpot. Every type of fuzzy toy imaginable hangs from the racks. And most have squeakers, strategically placed in the head, body, and tip of the tail. They're perfect.

Ignoring the flamingoes and dragons, Lisa selects toys representing animals she thinks will be familiar to Solomon. A fox, a squirrel, a rabbit, a chipmunk, a mallard duck, and a woodchuck are tossed into her shopping basket. She pulls a stuffed plush cat off the rack next, then changes her mind. Instead, she chooses a few duplicates—another squirrel, another rabbit, another duck. That'll be enough for now, she thinks. If she needs more, she'll come back. It's not like PetSmart's going anywhere.

Lisa drops the shopping bag filled with dog toys onto the kitchen island, then goes upstairs to look for a blanket to put in Solomon's shed. She pulls all the blankets from the top shelf of the linen closet and places them on the floor. She can't remember the last time she used any of them. As she unfolds each one, she checks for size and thickness. Most she folds neatly back up again, setting them aside for Goodwill.

The perfect blanket for Solomon needs to be thick, heavy enough to keep out the cold. It also has to be large enough for him to dig into a nest or burrow in. When she picks up the next-to-last blanket from the pile on the floor, she smiles. The blanket is blue, made of very dense wool, and, when she unfolds it, appears to be king-size. This one is perfect. Now the challenge will be finding the right time to get it into his shed

Lisa spends the next few hours waiting for a glimpse of Solomon passing by in a direction indicating he's headed away from the shed. It's mid-afternoon before she sees him. He passes by Ella's playhouse, then trots across the far end of the yard. Veering right, he heads down the hill. She wonders where he's off to. Is he going to his den under the porch? To the small beach beside the Coast Guard station? Maybe over to Jo's? What she hopes he's not doing is going for a quick stroll, then looping back to his shed. She knows this may be a very limited window of opportunity, and jumps on it.

Moments later, Lisa and Ella pull into the driveway of the abandoned house. Even though the quickest route to the shed is on foot, along the path Solomon normally uses as his cut-through, Lisa decides not to go that way. If he's already returned to the shed, she and Ella approaching from his preferred exit route will force him to escape via busy Main Street instead.

She worries about leaving their scent in too many places, especially in and around the shed. She doesn't want him to feel his safe place is no longer safe. Still, she believes providing Solomon with some warmth and comfort is worth the risk. Maybe she'll be able to figure out a way to get the blanket into the space without having to go inside.

"This place is spooky," Ella says, looking at the house.

"It does look kind of spooky, doesn't it? But I think it's just sad. Sad that its people moved away and nobody else moved in to love it."

"Why does Solomon want to live in a sad place?"

The question pierces.

"Because it's empty, sweetie, and because he feels safe here, away from people."

"I hope he finds a happy house to live in someday."

Lisa leans over, kisses Ella's head. "Me, too, sweetheart. Me, too."

They get out of the car and approach the shed. Lisa's sure he's not inside. If he were, he would've heard them by now and made a run for it.

"Okay, sweetie, let's go up to the door and see if we can get Solomon's blanket inside so he can be warm tonight."

When they arrive at the shed, Lisa looks through the window. She sees a small patch of floor devoid of junk, pumps her fist. "Yes!"

Ella peers into the shed, too. She sees nothing but a cold, dirty, messy space full of old broken things with pointy ends. To her, it looks like a horrible place to live.

"Why're you so happy, Mommy?"

Lisa points to the low-hung window with half the pane missing. "Because we don't have to go inside to leave Solomon his blanket. I can just toss it right through the window, right onto where the floor's clear. He might get nervous if he smells us in his hiding place."

"Oh … *now* I get it."

"Want to help me unfold the blanket?" Lisa asks.

They unfold the blanket and lay it on the ground. Lisa scoops it back up into her arms, arranging it into a nest shape. Her goal is for the blanket to land in a high heap when tossed through the window. That way, it'll be easy for Solomon to dig it into whatever shape he likes. She hopes that even with the blanket's human scents, Solomon won't hesitate to use the new addition to his environment.

"Okay, here goes," she tells Ella, then reaches through the window, aims carefully, and tosses the blanket. It falls just short of the hoped-for center of the cleared space. Still, it's close enough, and not resting on any dangerous objects. It's not worth a trip into the shed to adjust the location. The important thing is that he now has a blanket, and she has one less thing to worry about. Yes, Solomon lives alone in the sad house. That she can't change. At least not today. She's changed what she can, given him warmth. For now, it's the best she can do.

Within twenty feet of the shed, Solomon stops. He stands still, the fur along his spine rising. Then his nose hits the ground. His body zigzags in every direction, nose skimming the top of the leaf cover and then burrowing beneath it, senses gathering information. Sounds and visual clues fade, sometimes immediately. But scent lingers. And at the moment, the scent-processing part of his brain is frenetic, searching out every last trace of the left-behind.

He identifies two distinct scents. In some places they're separate, in other places co-mingled. They are familiar; he's caught regular whiffs of them while eating in his cut-through yard, or passing through it on his neighborhood rounds. He's not alarmed by the scents themselves. It's their being out of place that disturbs him. The information he takes in and processes, multiple layers of scents within scents, conveys no danger. Still, these smells he associates with somewhere else now permeate the area around the place he considers his, and he is wary.

Eventually he covers the entirety of the ground surrounding the shed, inhaling and exhaling, his mind and olfactory system on overdrive. Finally satisfied that there's no reason for concern, Solomon rises onto his hind legs, places his front paws on the window ledge, and jumps into the shed. He immediately notices the shape of something unfamiliar. It lies just past his feet, motionless and silent.

He pushes his nose against it, detects the same human scents he smelled outside. Those, and some other, unfamiliar scents, all mingled together. Solomon sniffs a bit more, then begins to dig and tug at the object. He pushes at the edges with his nose, digs some more. The digging and pushing and tugging continue until the object on the floor resembles a nest. He rolls on it, paws in the air, covering it with his own scent. Then he curls up tightly, the warmth of his new nest protecting him from the cold evening air to which he's become so accustomed.

The next morning, Solomon makes his way up the slope from his shed and across the yard to his food. As he approaches the bowl he notices something on the ground. He recognizes its shape as an animal he has sometimes picked up from the street and eaten. But he doesn't detect the same scent. It doesn't have any animal smell at all. Curious, he pushes at the animal with his nose, flips it over with a paw. It lies on the ground, motionless. He leaves it there and heads over to his food.

Solomon hears a scraping noise, and looks up at the house. He sees the woman's face, hears her voice. The sound of it, its variety of gentle, happy pitches, soothes him.

"Hi, Solomon. I hope your blanket kept you warm last night. And I hope you like your new rabbit toy. I don't know if you've ever had a toy, or even if you know how to play. But at least it'll keep you warm if you cuddle up with it at night."

When the voice stops, Solomon drops his head to eat. Today his food has broth. When he's finished eating, he runs his tongue along the bowl's edge, making sure he's left no speck of broth behind. Then he looks up at the window again. He sees the woman's face, but hears nothing. He waits to see if she'll speak again, but when the sounds do not resume he turns and heads back across the yard.

On the way past the fuzzy, motionless animal, he stops again. He lowers his head and picks the animal up. As his teeth close around the animal's middle, it squeaks loudly. Startled, he drops it. He pokes at it again with his nose, paws at it. He knows it's not alive. Why is it making noise? He picks it up again. Again it squeaks.

But this time he's not startled. The high-pitched squeals excite him, and he grabs the furry animal in his mouth, shakes it vigorously. He tosses it in the air, catches it, shakes it some more. It squeaks and squeals. He flings the toy animal up in the air a few more times, leaping around to catch it, tail wagging. Finally, he lowers himself to the ground and lies there, one front paw placed firmly, possessively, over the animal. Solomon pants, his heart beating hard against the ground. He trots over to the bowl of fresh water beside his food and drinks in rhythmic slurps, then returns to the toy. He picks it up around its neck and trots off in the direction of his shed, head high, tail up.

Lisa watches it all from the window. He does know how to play, she thinks. Does this mean he once had a home, a family who loved him? Or is play instinctual for a dog? She doesn't know. But she's mesmerized, unable to take her eyes off Solomon and his new toy. As he heads off, tail wagging and the plush brown rabbit toy dangling from his mouth, Lisa's eyes fill. It's been, she realizes, a very long time since she's felt this particular kind of joy.

Every few days, Solomon finds another furry animal lying near his food. Sometimes he plays with them, sometimes he doesn't. But he always takes them with him. And he now associates the scent of the human who feeds him with comfort, the sound of her voice with food. One morning after eating, he feels a strong sense of curiosity about this human. Abandoning his normal caution he crosses the yard and walks quietly up to the house, the place where the voice usually originates.

From where he stands he hears the voice, but just barely. He tracks it for a few feet, and then a few more, until he locates its source. He climbs a small set of steps onto the porch, walks over to the closest window, and looks inside. Unnoticed, he quietly observes the human and the small human beside her. They're smiling, and the human holds the small one against her. His instincts tell him the human is good, will never harm him. But there's something about the small human that draws him in. He stands utterly still, eyes boring into her.

Lisa and Ella sit on the floor in the den eating a late breakfast and watching cartoons, talking and laughing. It's a typical Saturday morning, until Ella feels the weight of a stare. She turns her head to the bank of windows.

"Mommy," she whispers. "Solomon's on the porch. He's looking at us!"

Lisa looks out the windows and there he is, gazing in at them. She tries not to look him in the eyes, mindful of what she's been told by Beth and Leslie. But she can't help it. It's as if some force of nature pulls her eyes to the exact place she doesn't want them to go. But Solomon stands his ground.

"Yes, he is. Let's just sit here quietly and let him peek through the window, okay? We don't want to scare him."

Ella nods and sits motionless on the floor, looking at Solomon. He returns her gaze with an expression she interprets as curiosity. And then, because she has no other means to communicate, she smiles at him. When he smiles back at her in his dog way, her six-year-old heart melts. Solomon remains on the porch for another minute, maybe two, then turns and walks back down the steps and into the yard. Ella and Lisa watch him trot briskly away, tail held high.

For Lisa, everything with regard to Solomon is different now. Those few minutes he stood on the porch looking in at them are going to be, she knows, among the most consequential of her life. She'll never forget the look in his eyes: a mixture of love, longing, hope, wisdom, and curiosity. In that look was every wonderful thing that Solomon is. Everything he'll be to her and Ella, everything her family will be to him. She sees it all so plainly now.

Solomon doesn't belong in Maine. Lisa understands, as completely as she's ever understood anything, that she and Ella are the purpose of Solomon's amazing journey. She vividly remembers that night back in mid-April when she'd stood on the same porch Solomon had just stood on. Arms open, head thrown back, praying to whatever powers might be listening for the love she needed.

And the very next day, Solomon had appeared on her lawn. The Universe got it right this time, she thinks. He's everything she asked for, everything she needs, in the purest of forms. And her family, her small human pack, is everything Solomon needs. They are each other's destiny. It's not just an imagining, a fantasy. It's true and real, as clear to her now as the early stars had been on that chilly night back in April.

Sixteen

Indian Summer is making a late, unexpected appearance in Hull Village. Lisa and Leslie sit on the steps of Lisa's back porch, soaking the sun into their bones. As always, they're discussing their favorite topic: Solomon.

"He came right up onto the porch and looked through the window at us. Almost as if he was scoping us out, you know? Trying to see what it would be like to be inside, to live with us."

"That's amazing. I don't think he's ever done anything like that," Leslie says.

"I know."

They're quiet for a few moments, letting that vision of Solomon, that moment everyone would have considered impossible just days earlier, linger. It feels too fragile, too precious, to layer words over. Lisa breaks the silence, her voice quiet but determined.

"I want him. So does Ella, and Dave's on board, too."

Leslie is taken aback. No one has any idea how Solomon will behave around cats or children. And his previous experiences living with people haven't ended well. She worries that living with the Parsons family will be no different. Still, he *has* taken the surprising step of walking up onto the porch to observe Lisa and Ella close up. That has to mean something. She's just not sure what.

"You do? What about how he might react to Ella, and the cats?"

"I don't know how he'll react to the cats. I'll have to be very careful and thoughtful about how I introduce them to each other. But I'm not worried about Ella at all. The way he looked at her through the window … I don't know, it's hard to describe. But I could see in his eyes that he'd never hurt her."

Leslie hadn't been there, so can't disagree. And after every bizarre thing that's gone wrong trying to recover him, she's convinced that Solomon's in Hull Village for a reason. Maybe this family, this home, really is what he's been looking for all along. It's just taken a while for everyone, maybe even Solomon, to realize it.

"Well, it'd be amazing for Solomon, and for you guys, too, if that's how this all turns out."

"I do think it'll end up that way. I really believe he's meant to be with us."

Before Leslie has a chance to respond, Solomon appears from the bushes. He turns his head, looks pointedly in their direction, then slowly crosses the yard and heads up the hill.

"I don't think I've ever seen him move that slowly," Leslie says. "It's as if he wanted to make sure we saw him, wanted us to know he'd been hiding in the bushes, listening to everything we said."

Goosebumps rise along Lisa's arms. "I know. I thought the exact same thing. It's like he wanted us to know he heard us, that he understood."

They have no proof to support their interpretation of Solomon's behavior. But they agree this is one of those experiences for which proof is unnecessary. They saw what they saw, know what they know.

"So, I guess we should work on coming up with a new plan, see if we can recover him. Somehow. I think you'll need the okay from Hope to adopt him, though. Since Underhound Railroad brought him up from Georgia, and he was never adopted, I'm pretty sure that technically he's still theirs."

It hasn't occurred to Lisa that she'd need permission to adopt Solomon, or that someone might refuse to let her do so. Not until now. Isn't a happy ending what everyone wants for him? She and her family *are* that happy ending. She knows it. Would someone with the power to grant that happy ending to Solomon actually refuse to do so? She shivers despite the sun's warmth.

"Do you want me to talk with Hope?" Leslie asks. "We hit it off when we first spoke. I think if the situation's presented in the right way, she'll be open to considering it."

"I appreciate the offer, Leslie. But I want to talk with her myself." No one else had seen the look in Solomon's eyes as he gazed at her and Ella through the window. There's no one who can better articulate how she knows what she knows, or why Solomon belongs with her family.

"I get that. But if you change your mind, the offer stands."

Lisa smiles, and the conversation turns to possible ways to recover Solomon. Whatever they do next needs to not only be new to him, but simple. No more magnetic or battery-operated parts that fail inexplicably. Just old-fangled, basic components. For the past week, Lisa's been working on an idea, refining it down to the smallest detail. She thinks it might succeed.

"I've been working on a plan. Want to hear it?" she asks Leslie.

"Absolutely."

Lisa outlines the plan step by step, from bringing Solomon inside to successfully integrating him into her family.

"So? What do you think?" she asks.

It's a simple plan, requiring nothing but a few basics and some time. Which is exactly why Leslie thinks it might work. She still has some reservations about what could happen once Solomon is recovered and inside Lisa's house. But Lisa has thought carefully about how she'll introduce Solomon to his new environment. And she's not naively assuming he'll blend right in with her family, as if the last two years hadn't happened. For Leslie, Lisa's understanding of the realities and potential challenges of the situation goes a long way toward mitigating her concerns.

"I actually think it could work," Leslie says. "And I think we need to talk with Beth and the ARL, ask for a moratorium on trying to recover Solomon. The best thing we can do for this dog, in my opinion, is to let him find his family. At his own pace, and on his own terms."

An hour after her conversation with Leslie, Beth's mind is still reeling. There are so many aspects of their discussion to consider, to try to make sense of. But there's one thing that keeps bubbling up, pushing everything else below the surface. It's the fact that Solomon actually walked right onto Lisa's porch and stared in the window at her and Ella. Stood there while they all looked at each other. It's shaken up everything she thought she knew about Solomon's behavior.

She can't find a single logical reason, from a dog's perspective, for Solomon to be standing on Lisa's porch. It's not where his food and water are, or anything else of typical value to a dog. At this point, she agrees with Leslie: Solomon's journey isn't a random meandering south through New England. It has a purpose, and that purpose is to find his family, the place he belongs. The more Beth deconstructs it all, the more sense it makes. Still, she finds Lisa's plan to recover Solomon concerning.

It's not the mechanics of it that have her worried. Those, she thinks, have a good chance of success. The more complicated, professional methods they've tried so far haven't worked, so why not try something simple? The fewer moving parts, the less opportunity for screw-ups. And the plan provides a timetable that allows Solomon to come inside when he's ready. In a way that respects his dignity. Dignity matters to dogs; anyone who thinks otherwise knows nothing of the canine spirit. And if the plan fails, no harm done. No component gone awry that could potentially spook Solomon into going on the run again. Yup, the plan in and of itself is fine, Beth thinks.

It's the post-recovery aspect of it that's troubling her. For starters, no one knows how Solomon will react to being inside again. She shares Leslie's concerns about Lisa's cats, but doesn't think he'll harm Ella. He's never shown aggressive tendencies. Not in his foster home, not at the D'Arpino's, not at the ARL. Beth has no reason to believe his temperament has changed. She hopes she's right. Because if she's not, that'll be it. Biting a child will automatically make him unadoptable. He'll almost surely have to be put down, an outcome she has no idea how she'd ever learn to live with.

And then, assuming all goes well inside the house, there's the issue of the yard not being fenced. A dog who's been living on his own for a long period of time has highly developed startle responses and trigger reactions. The dog's family has no way of knowing or anticipating those triggers until they're set off. And in most cases, dogs respond to their startle triggers by doing what they've learned provides their best chance for survival. They run. But this problem can be solved by fencing the yard. If the ground's already too hard, Lisa could keep Solomon on-leash until spring and put up the fence then.

So. One problem solved. And, in theory, she agrees with Leslie and Lisa on scaling back their recovery efforts, giving something low-tech a try. But still. Pulling back even a little on a dog needing to be brought to safety causes a certain amount of cognitive dissonance. Especially when that dog is Solomon. She understands she'll know no peace until Solomon is safe, living happily with a family. But pulling back on efforts to achieve this still seems, in some ways, counterintuitive.

In other ways, though, it seems exactly right. Looking back at those odd recovery failures, she now believes they were about Solomon's need to choose his own family. To end his journey on his own terms. She hadn't fully understood this. Not for a long time, not in the way she does now. And neither had anyone else obsessed, in only the best-intentioned of ways, with recovering Solomon.

She sighs. "Okay," she says to the empty room. "I get it."

It's time for them to let Lisa do her thing, and see what happens.

Hope sits on the sofa, meditative, listening deeply to the argument between her heart and mind over Lisa's request to adopt Solomon. She cups her hands around a mug of warm herbal tea, looks at her own aging dogs curled up on their beds by the wood-burning stove. Her love for them is so intense. She'll do whatever it takes to help them live long, happy, healthy lives. Even if it means going broke in the process. Her dogs are the most amazing gifts, and she cherishes them.

Every dog deserves what her dogs have. It's why she went out to Utah all those years ago to work at Best Friends Animal Sanctuary, why she became involved with Underhound Railroad. Finding loving homes for dogs is her passion. It may not be her sole purpose in life, but it's undeniably one of the most central. And she very much wants to help Solomon find his people, his home. So why this hesitation, this back and forth of emotion and logic?

It has nothing to do with Lisa herself. Hope's eyes had filled when Lisa told her about the plush toys she leaves out for him, the thick blanket she placed in his shed. In Hope's mind those actions are enormous, telling. Lisa clearly loves Solomon, and the care she provides for him goes far beyond simply providing food and water. Hope wonders if Solomon somehow understands that. Is that why he walked up onto the porch to look in at Lisa and Ella? Does he recognize that he's finally found what he's spent almost two full circles around the sun searching for? She wishes she knew.

Her reservations have everything to do with her own excruciating experience of tracking Solomon through the Kittery winter after he bolted from Steve and Carmen. She knows how smart this dog is. Because of his history he's absolutely a flight risk, always will be. If he runs again he'll likely never be recovered. And this, really, is what's at the heart of Hope's conflicting feelings: Lisa has admitted she has no plans to fence in her yard.

Hope isn't worried about the possibility of Solomon killing Lisa's cats or harming Ella. Not at all. The Solomon she knows doesn't have an ounce of aggression in him, and she believes that other than intentional training or extreme cruelty by humans, nothing can turn a dog who's gentle by nature aggressive. Her only real concern is that without a fenced-in yard, Solomon might escape again. She's explained to Lisa that she'll have to keep him on leash, always, if she doesn't have a fenced space for him to run loose in. Lisa seems to understand, doesn't have an issue with the restriction.

But does she really understand? Hope knows firsthand the many quirks of rescue dogs, the odd and unexpected things that trigger their flight response. In her experience, everyone who adopts a flight-risk dog agrees to abide by the always-on-leash rule. Eventually, though, as the dog settles in and bonds with the family, they're lulled into believing it's now okay to let their dog off leash. Sometimes they get lucky, but sometimes their lapse in judgment ends in tragedy.

Her heart, she fears, will literally break if Solomon disappears again. And she wonders how many lives he has. He's been amazingly lucky so far, and she questions how much longer his luck will last. Can she, as the person ultimately responsible for Solomon, agree in good conscience to let someone without a fenced-in yard adopt him? She doesn't know. What she does know is that if she gives her permission and something happens to Solomon, she'll never forgive herself. Never get out from under the weight of her guilt. Not ever. And that terrifies her.

And yet.

Her mind can't erase the images of Lisa carefully selecting and leaving soft, cuddly toys for him, placing the blanket in his shed, faithfully feeding him every day, talking softly to him when he shows up for his meals. And then there's the image most indelibly etched into her mind: the one of Solomon standing on the porch, gazing through the window at Lisa and Ella. Something about that image is gut-wrenching. To her, it defines his entire life. A life lived on the outside looking in. A life of observing people through walls both literal and figurative. But in taking those steps onto Lisa's porch, Hope wonders if he's trying to tell them he's ready to be inside, looking out.

By the time Hope finishes her tea, the decision about the rest of Solomon's life has been made. After everything he's been through, if living in Hull Village with the Parsons family is what he chooses, who is she to say no? She calls Lisa, tells her yes. If and when Solomon is recovered, she can adopt him, with Underhound Railroad's gratitude.

Seventeen

In the beginning there's just "Lisa's plan." It consists of a series of intentionally uncomplicated steps, simple enough for a child to understand and participate in. Lisa has assigned Ella the role of look-out, complete with code-word and walkie-talkie, and now Ella perches on a stool at the kitchen island. Leaning in, she watches closely as Lisa removes the walkie-talkies from their packaging and reads the assembly directions.

"Mommy, are we going to bring Solomon in the house today?"

"I don't think so. He has to decide for himself that he's ready to come inside and live with us, and that'll probably take a little time."

"Why? Doesn't Solomon want to live here?"

"I think he does, sweetheart. He just needs to be sure he trusts us."

"I can't wait 'til he does!"

"Me, too." Lisa can barely remember what it was like to go through a day without worrying about Solomon. She looks forward to rediscovering that former life.

The walkie-talkies are ready for action. Lisa opens the coat closet and pulls out a plastic shopping bag, the logo of the local hardware store splashed across it. Inside the bag is the rest of the plan's equipment. There's not much; a large door latch and a long, strong rope. Those two items—along with the walkie-talkies, time, and infinite patience—are the extent of what her plan to bring Solomon inside requires.

Off of Lisa's living room is a sunny, three-season back porch that runs the width of the house. Beneath it is a large enclosed space, its footprint identical to that of the porch above. The enclosure's floor is packed dirt, and the front and side walls are wooden lattice, painted forest green on the outside and left unpainted on the inside. Lisa has affixed floor-to-ceiling chicken wire to the enclosure's inside walls. Throughout the space, cat perches, small wooden ramps, and feline jungle-gyms made from tree branches rest along the walls.

This is the cats' indoor-outdoor playground. They love the illusion of being outside, and Lisa loves knowing they're safe from harm while they enjoy that illusion. She hopes the cats will forgive her for shutting down their play area for a while. Unfortunately for them, this space is where she intends to move Solomon's food and water, the place where he'll come inside when he's ready.

By Lisa's figuring, the plan might take a month, maybe two. Solomon's food and water will be moved in increments across the backyard, closer and closer to the enclosure beneath the porch. Assuming that process goes well, his bowls will eventually be placed inside the enclosure. At that point, the outside door to the space will be left open for him to come and go freely.

Once Solomon takes his first steps inside to eat, his food will be gradually moved, farther and farther into the space, until it's just beyond the corner leading into the most tucked-away part of the enclosure. Lisa wants him to be as far from the door as possible, but thinks he might not go for his food being quite so far inside. And really, just a bit beyond that corner will be far enough. She's sure of it. Ella's lookout point is a window that provides a clear view into that section of the space. As long as she can see any part of him in that area, they'll be fine.

When Solomon's eating inside on a regular basis, they'll begin keeping watch during his mealtimes with their walkie-talkies. Ella will be at her designated window, Lisa at another window midway along the porch; the window that's directly above the enclosure's door. Or somewhere nearby. That's the beauty of the walkie-talkies. As long as Ella's at her spot, Lisa can be anywhere on the first floor. As soon as Ella sees him at his food bowl, she'll say the code word: "Solomon." Lisa will race to her own designated window if she's not already there. Then she'll pull on the long rope attached to the enclosure door's new metal latch. The rope runs tautly up the side of the house and through the window and, when pulled, will close and latch the door. And Solomon, finally, will be safe inside.

At least, that's how she envisions it all in her mind. It's possible, of course, that something will go awry. The walkie-talkies will malfunction. The thick rope will break. The well-fitting door will stick, or the oiled latch will miss its mark. The things that have gone wrong with the previous attempts at recovering Solomon have been so bizarre—just like a stuck door or snapping rope would be. But Lisa's convinced the things that torpedoed earlier recovery efforts happened for a specific reason. And that reason was to prevent Solomon from ending up on yet another path chosen for him, with no way to control his own destiny other than to run.

If this is where he's meant to live, and he's able to end his journey when he's ready, nothing will go wrong. And if things do go wrong, she'll know he isn't meant to be here after all. Which will be hard to accept. She's already so emotionally invested in Solomon, in his future life with her family. Letting go of her conviction that Solomon's meant to be with them will take every ounce of emotional strength she possesses. But she'll do it, do whatever it takes to help him find the place he belongs.

His food and water aren't quite where they were the day before, and Solomon notices the slight shift immediately. He sniffs at the grass around the bowl, then at the food itself. He recognizes the scent of it as his usual meal. It's just not in its usual place. Still, the bowls aren't so far away from their previous location as to be unsettling. And he's hungry. He takes a quick look around, then plunges in.

As he eats he pricks his ears up, listening to the soft voice coming from above him. He's used to the voice now. It's become a part of his daily routine, connected to one of his favorite things—food.

"'Morning, Solomon. I hope you have a happy, safe day. Things'll be better soon, I promise." Lisa continues speaking to Solomon, saying whatever pops into her head.

He sinks into the feeling of comfort he experiences in the presence of the light, gentle voice, and continues to eat. His food now gone, he turns to the water bowl, noisily laps at the water. He runs his tongue, still wet from the water, in a single swipe over his mouth and nose, then looks up toward the source of the voice. He sees the human in the window, watching him. He returns her gaze calmly, then turns and trots off. He's just past the side of the house, approaching the quiet street, when he hears a muffled scraping sound followed by a slight bang. Both the sound and scent of the human abruptly disappear.

The November days pass, and Lisa regularly moves Solomon's food and water just a bit closer to the enclosure beneath the porch. Lisa knows the decision to trust her enough to want to come inside, to eat in a secluded part of the enclosure, is up to Solomon. Still, it's harder than ever for her to think of him outside on his own. He's not just Solomon anymore. He's Solomon Parsons. And members of the Parsons family live inside, warm and loved. She wonders if she might be able to speed things up. Nothing drastic. Just moving his food a bit further every day, instead of every few days, getting it to the enclosure's door faster. It might not change anything, she knows, because it'll still be up to him to go inside when he's ready. But she thinks it's worth a try. If he seems disturbed by it, she can always slow things down.

The next morning, she moves the bowls six inches from their previous location. Then she goes inside to watch for him from the window. As he approaches from the far end of the backyard she cracks open the window, letting him catch her scent. She wants him to become as used to her smell and the sound of her voice as possible. And to associate both with having his needs met.

Solomon ambles across the yard in the direction of his food. When he arrives at the bowls' previous location, he drops his nose to the ground. He roots around in the short grass, sniffing a small area, then takes a few quick steps over to the bowl. He sniffs that, too, then begins to lap the food from the bowl. He hears the woman's voice, but doesn't look up. Instead, he continues eating, listening.

"Hi, Solomon. I hope you kept warm last night. You're a very special boy, and I love you. Ella loves you, too, and we want you to live with us."

His food gone, he sniffs around in the grass for any wayward morsels. He can still catch the human's scent, but the voice is silent. He looks up at the window, then turns and trots back across the yard.

Lisa watches Solomon head off to wherever it is he goes after he eats, watches until he disappears from sight. Excited and relieved that he didn't seem disturbed by the slightly different location of his bowls, she does some mental math. By her calculations, moving the bowls a foot a day—six inches in the morning, six inches in the evening—should get Solomon to the door of the enclosure by Thanksgiving. If only her yard weren't so huge. If only the starting point—the trap—had been closer to the house. But, that's what she has to work with.

And so she patiently keeps at it, the process maddeningly slow. She knows it has to be this way if her plan is going to succeed. But the waiting. The waiting is so much harder than she'd ever imagined it would be.

Sometime in the middle of November, during a conversation with Leslie, things shift, becoming more urgent.

"They're talking about trying to dart him again," Leslie says.

"What? *Why*? I thought they agreed to back off for a while and let me try things my way."

"I know. They did. But I think they're having second thoughts. The concern that he might be aggressive toward Ella or the cats seems to have popped up again. And they're thinking that maybe it's not a great idea to let someone inexperienced try to recover this particular dog. Not that I agree. I'm just saying."

Lisa's stomach churns. Why is there such fear that Solomon will be aggressive? She sees his body language daily, saw the way he looked at Ella through the window for those brief moments. He's not going to be aggressive. She's certain of it. But how to convince Team Solomon, when so many things have already gone sideways with this dog? She's not sure the words exist.

"What worries me," Leslie continues, "is that if they dart him he may bite someone when he comes to, just out of fear. It happens sometimes."

"But they're experienced with this kind of thing. They'll be able to tell the difference between true aggression and dart-related aggression, right?"

"Right. But for some reason I just have a bad feeling about it."

"Okay, so let's say they manage to dart him this time. He completely and totally freaks out when the tranquilizer wears off, and attacks someone. What then?"

For a long moment, Leslie says nothing. The answer to Lisa's question is so inconceivable she can barely bring herself to voice it. But Lisa loves Solomon, is planning to adopt him. She has a right to know.

"They may decide the best option is to put him down." Leslie speaks quietly, but her words shake Lisa as profoundly as if they'd been an explosion. *Put him down?* No. She will not allow that to happen.

"Then I have to get him first," Lisa says.

"Hopefully, that's what'll happen."

"Hopefully." Lisa looks down at her hands, feeling the first bit of self-doubt, of second-guessing. Her thumb pushes rhythmically at the cuticle on her right ring finger.

She looks back up at Leslie. "But what if they're right, and I've completely misjudged him, or misinterpreted his behavior? What if he comes inside and *is* aggressive? I think we need a back-up plan."

"Honestly? I think your gut feeling about him is right on target. But no harm in having a back-up plan." Leslie sighs. "Right now, I'd give almost anything to see into the future. I'm serious. Almost anything."

"Me, too."

Now there are two plans to help bring Solomon to the end of his travels. One is Plan A, the one everyone knows about. Lisa still believes it will work, that ultimately all will be well. But she's not willing to proceed without a back-up plan. Not anymore, not when she knows what's potentially at stake. So, after much discussion, she and Leslie come up with Plan B.

They hope to never have to use it, intend to share it with no one. But it's there if they need it. Like Lisa's plan, which they now call Plan A, Plan B is simple: If Plan A succeeds, they'll wait a week before telling anyone Solomon's come inside. That week will give them time to see if he's aggressive. If he is, he'll have time to adjust, to show his best, true self. If after a week he's still aggressive, they'll drive him out to a sanctuary in Utah, where he'll be able to live out his life in a caring, loving environment.

When Hope gave her approval for Solomon's adoption, it was Lisa's understanding that once she has him, he's hers. She assumes there'll be some formal papers to sign, but even without the papers, she and Leslie believe Plan B breaks no laws. But they also believe it's in no one's best interest for them to put the details of it up for discussion. It is, after all, only a Plan B. Why waste time and energy on dissecting something they're likely never going to use? Plan A, Lisa's plan, is probably going to work out just fine. Why give anyone the opportunity to further doubt it, and her, by revealing the existence of Plan B?

Eighteen

Hull Village is experiencing an early cold snap. The arctic air that some-times sweeps down from Canada has arrived for what Lisa hopes will be an abbreviated visit. Combined with the damp ocean air, it creates a particular type of bone-permeating cold that she sometimes can't shake until late spring.

And the early arrival of the cold increases her concerns about Solomon. Is he warm enough in his shed, even with his thick blanket and cuddly toys? What if, by the time the snow begins to fall, he's still outside? If he chooses the tight and likely warmer space beneath the porch on Andrew Avenue and there's a major snowstorm, could the accumulated snow block his exit, or the holes in the lattice? And if so, could he suffocate?

She pushes these thoughts away, attempts to reassure herself. He's survived two very cold New England winters, will almost certainly be fine. Still, her worrying for him is constant. The thought of him outside on his own in the damp bitter cold eats at her, devouring large portions of her energy. She wishes she could gauge Solomon's level of trust in her. How much longer until he's ready to eat inside the enclosure, to live as an indoor dog with a family? What would happen if she moved his food and water within thirty feet of the enclosure and continued the current process from there? She decides to find out. The worst that can happen is that he won't eat there until she moves it all back to where it was.

The cold wind whistles through the cracks in the shed's clapboards and blows in through the window, carrying with it the distinct smell of salt. The scent of the ocean air is one of Solomon's favorite things. He often pauses his travels along the stretches of sand by the water to stand facing the waves, nose lifted high, nostrils working overtime. The smell sends him racing down the beach, his dog smile wide, chasing after anything in his path.

But tonight, he finds no pleasure in it. He burrows tightly and deeply into his blanket, his vulnerable nose buried protectively beneath a foreleg. His plush toys lie against and beneath him, their squeakers sounding each time he shifts position. Solomon's body knows winter is approaching, and his short hair has begun to grow thicker in response. Still, it's not enough. He curls his shivering body tighter. After a while, his body generates enough heat to relax his muscles. The shivering stops, and only then does he sleep.

The next morning, Lisa observes Solomon's approach. She's curious to see his reaction to the repositioning of his food and water. The way he stops short, looks furtively at his surroundings, sends a rush of heat through her body and up into her head. It dances around her scalp, tingles the roots of her hair. Has she moved his bowls too far, far enough to unnerve him, undo the trust she's worked so hard to build?

"C'mon, Solomon … it's okay. Come eat your food."

She whispers the words as if they were a prayer. And perhaps they are. Because although she hasn't opened the window, he seems to hear her. The words are barely spoken when Solomon apparently decides to trust the situation and lowers his head into the bowl.

She lifts the window to talk to him while he eats. The air drifting in is cold, and she wraps her shawl scarf tighter around her body, encasing her hands in its folds.

"Hi, Solomon. I hope you're staying warm on these cold nights…and I hope you'll be ready to come live with us soon. We love you so much, and want you to be safe and warm in your forever home."

She rambles on, a series of unrelated thoughts floating in and out of her mind, much of it meaningless even to her. It's not the meaning of it that's important, though. What matters is that he continues to hear the sound of her voice, continues to associate it with something he can depend on. Something he can trust. But is Solomon experiencing her voice in the way she hopes? She has nothing she can point to as proof.

And then, unexpectedly, she does. What she sees doesn't last long. But there's no mistaking it for an involuntary motion, a twitch in response to the cold. It's wholly intentional. For the first time since she's been feeding him and speaking to him from her window, Solomon looks up at her and wags his tail. Has he finally recognized in her voice whatever it is he's spent the past two years searching for? She doesn't know. But she does know that the sight of Solomon's wagging tail, however brief, has brought her something she's in deep and desperate need of: joy. True, unadulterated joy.

The final leg of Solomon's journey begins with a trail of treats. Lisa has scattered a line of particularly aromatic treats leading from his food's previous location to its new spot just inside the enclosure. She watches from her lookout window, waiting for Solomon's arrival. Will he go in? She has no idea what to expect from him. But if he doesn't go in today, she'll try again tomorrow. And the day after that. She'll try until his refusal to eat inside tells her it's time to move slower, tells her he's not ready.

Solomon bounds up the incline behind the shed. He's hungry, and heads straight across the yard toward his morning meal. But when he arrives at the usual location, he doesn't see his food. He smells it, though.

It's coming from farther across the yard. And he smells something else, too; a strong, appetizing scent coming from the ground. He drops his nose to the ground and finds several small nuggets of soft, chewy meat not far from his front paws. He eats them, then continues forward, snuffling through the grass, scarfing down the treats he finds scattered there.

When the treat trail ends, Solomon is standing in front of his food bowl. It's right on the other side of the doorway, inside the enclosure. The smell of the food makes him salivate. He stretches his neck out and then his paws, tries to reach the bowl without stepping inside. Unable to do so, he stands for a few moments outside the doorway. Then he turns around and disappears through the hedge, still hungry.

Solomon's refusal to eat from inside the enclosure doesn't surprise Lisa. She feels bad that he didn't get to have his morning meal. At least he ate the treats. But now it's late afternoon, time for his dinner. Unless he's managed to hunt down or scavenge up some food, she expects he'll be back soon. She settles down by the window to wait for him. Before long, she notices him at the edge of the yard.

He seems nervous. Crossing the yard, he stops frequently, glances around. She watches as he drops his nose into the short grass. Again he finds and wolfs down the trail of treats leading to his food. Again he stands in front of the doorway, his food just inside. Again he waits, looks, listens. This time, he crosses the threshold. He must've gulped down his food like he hadn't eaten in days, Lisa thinks. She's never seen him eat and leave so quickly.

Now that Solomon's gone inside, eaten, and exited without negative consequences, Lisa hopes he'll be less nervous about eating there. At least the treat trail seems to be a hit. She's confident that as he becomes familiar with his new eating situation, he'll follow the treats farther and farther inside to his food. And when that happens, she'll know he's finally ready to become part of her family.

On Thanksgiving, Lisa prepares a special meal for Solomon. She's so grateful for him. Grateful for his daily presence, for the things he's taught her about resilience, following her heart, and living life on her own terms. In his utterly dependable comings and goings, he's restored her faith in constancy. One day soon she'll be able to express her gratitude to him in so many ways. But for now, the best she can do is include him in the family's—*his* family's—feast.

Ella comes into the kitchen.

"What are you doing, Mommy?"

"Getting Solomon's Thanksgiving dinner ready to take out to him."

"Does he get to have everything? Even pie?"

Lisa laughs. "No pie. And no cranberry sauce, either. I don't think sugar's good for him. He's having turkey, sweet potatoes, carrots, and some green beans." As she verbally ticks off each component of Solomon's dinner, Lisa places it into his bowl.

"And then, because Solomon likes his food mixed together, I'm going to stir it all up before I bring it out to him."

"Can I come with you?"

"Of course, sweetie. Go put on your jacket and we'll take it out to him together."

She watches Ella's back disappear through the door, hears her rummaging around in the coat closet, pulling her jacket off its hanger. When Ella returns to the kitchen, she's fully zipped into her pink jacket. Her hood is pulled up over her head, and strands of electrically-charged blond hair stick to her face. Her cheeks are flushed from the heat of her body encased in a jacket and hood in the middle of the still-warm kitchen. Lisa can't help smiling at the wondrous little person who is her daughter.

"Ready?"

Ella nods.

Lisa gathers together an empty bowl, a bottle of water, and a bag of treats, then hands them to Ella.

"Can you carry these for me?"

"Yup."

Lisa puts on her own jacket, then picks up Solomon's Thanksgiving dinner bowl from the counter.

"Okay, let's go!"

They make their way down the basement stairs, through the basement, into the enclosure, then out into the cold.

"Let's put Solomon's food down right here." The spot she indicates is well into the enclosure. "And his water here, next to his food. Want to pour his water for him?"

Lisa watches Ella open the plastic bottle and carefully pour the water into the bowl.

"I didn't spill any. Not even one drop! Can we throw the treats now?"

This is Ella's favorite part of setting out Solomon's food. It reminds her of Hansel and Gretel, when Hansel threw the white pebbles in the path to show them the way back home.

Lisa hands Ella the treat bag. "Here you go!"

Ella starts the trail at the bowl. She moves to the doorway, then out the door to the center of the backyard, dropping a line of treats until the bag is empty. Treat trail set, they go inside. They settle in by the window that provides the best view of Solomon's feeding area. It's an obstructed view, but there's not a better one. Once he's farther in, maybe ten feet from where his food and water are now, they'll be able to see him perfectly.

Solomon arrives shortly after Lisa and Ella take their place by the window. They watch as he walks across the yard, stopping to pick up treats along the way.

"There's Solly, Mommy," Ella whispers.

"Let's hope he's hungry."

Solomon approaches the doorway. He stops, looks around, listens; his usual routine before eating. Apparently satisfied with his surroundings, he walks inside and finds his Thanksgiving dinner. He doesn't rush through this meal. In fact, he takes longer than usual to finish. Is he beginning to consider her home a place of safety, worthy of his trust? Lisa wonders. After all his running, that she's gained even a measure of his trust seems almost miraculous.

A sudden profound gratitude overcomes her. She's so grateful for her life, despite all its current mess and uncertainty. Grateful for her family, grateful for the child snuggled up against her, grateful for this dog who's unexpectedly come into their lives.

"Happy Thanksgiving, Solomon," she whispers as he finishes off the last of his holiday meal. "Things will be different next year. For all of us."

Solomon hops through the broken window and into his shed. He digs at his blanket, then curls up on top of it with his toys. His belly is still full and heavy from his late afternoon meal. Feeling satiated and warm, he falls asleep almost immediately. Before long he begins to whine slightly, paws twitching. The sides of his mouth pull back and slightly upward as his tail thumps gently against the floor. He exhales audibly. Then his body becomes still, and he sleeps deeply, dreamlessly.

Nineteen

The morning after Thanksgiving Lisa and Ella sit at the dining room table, drinking hot chocolate, while Ella dictates her Christmas list for Santa. It's a long list, but not long enough to make Lisa consider hitting the malls on Black Friday. Instead, she uses the day to write out her holiday to-do lists. Lists of Christmas gifts for family, friends, and cats. Lists of holiday food treats to buy, lists of decorations and lights to be unpacked and put up. And this year, there's a new list: a list with SOLOMON written boldly across the top.

Her gut tells her Solomon's going to decide to come in from the cold any day now. He's following the treat trail to his food and water in the enclosure's back area, far enough in for Ella to see him from her lookout point in the dining room. But Lisa wants him to go even farther in. She wants to be sure he's completely comfortable inside before she lifts the window and pulls the rope that will latch the enclosure's door. It's not time yet. But soon. Very soon. She plans to be ready for him when that moment comes—his space all set up, his Christmas gifts purchased.

At the moment, though, the only thing written on Solomon's list is his name. He'll of course need food, a bed, toys, a collar, leashes, and dedicated food and water bowls. But she's never had a dog, has no idea which type or brand of any of these items is best. She attaches Ella's Christmas list for Santa to the refrigerator door with a couple of reindeer magnets, and puts the other lists away. Then she calls Hope for advice on Solomon's list.

A few hours later, Lisa pushes a shopping cart through the aisles at the pet store. Inside the cart is a warm, thick dog bed. On top of the bed, there's a thirty-five-pound bag of specialty kibble, and a ten-pound bag of a different brand. Just in case he doesn't like the one Hope recommended. Piled on top of the kibble bags are two cases of dog food cans.

And there are toys. Fuzzy toys with squeakers, stuffie toys, flat toys. She's thrown in a few heavy-duty rubber chew toys, a couple of rope toys. Her favorites, though, are the puzzle toys, meant to be stuffed with treats the dog has to figure out how to remove. She has a feeling Solomon will love those puzzle toys, even though it probably won't take him very long to figure them out.

Also in the cart are a couple of stainless steel bowls for food and water. She won't use them right away. It might be better, she thinks, to continue using the bowls he's accustomed to. At least for the first couple of weeks. But once he settles in, she wants him to have brand new bowls bought just for him.

The leashes draped over the toys, food, and bowls are thick and tightly woven. When Lisa spoke with Hope the day before, Hope had been adamant about both the leashes and the collar.

"Two leashes, super strong. He should be double leashed when you bring him outside, at least for the first couple of months. A leash clipped to his harness, and a leash clipped to his collar. If one of the leashes breaks, you'll still have him. And absolutely no retractable leash. Ever. They're dangerous."

"Got it. Two super-strong, non-retractable leashes. What about the collar and the harness?"

"For the collar, only get a martingale. It's what he has on now; he was transported wearing it. PetSmart and Petco both sell them. All dogs should have martingale collars, really, but especially flight-risk dogs."

"Why a martingale?"

"Because the dog can't slip out of it. Martingale harnesses are great, too. But any kind of strong, well-fitting harness he can't slip out of is fine."

"Ah. Okay."

"I've also been thinking it'd probably be a good idea to put a GPS on him. Especially since you're not planning to fence in your yard."

"I don't plan to let him off-leash anywhere, even in the yard. But I'll give it some thought."

In the end, though, she decides a GPS isn't necessary. The super-strong leashes, martingale, and harness Hope advised should be enough.

Lisa pushes her cart into the collars and harnesses aisle. The pet store has a limited selection of martingale collars. Lisa chooses a red one that looks like the right size for Solomon's neck, then tosses it into the shopping cart. She knows he needs a new collar. But there's a part of her that feels sentimental about that old, crusty collar of his. It's the only thing that's been with him for the entirety of his journey. She moves on to the harness section. There are more options here, and it takes longer to make her selection. She adds her final purchase, a royal blue harness, to the cart. She's ready now. Whenever he is.

When Lisa returns home, she lugs Solomon's things down into the basement. She puts his bed in an area not far from the furnace. After all the nights Solomon has slept outside in the cold, she wants his bed to go in the warmest place possible. She lays a few fuzzy toys at one end of the bed, then stacks his bowls, kibble bags, and cans on a work table. The leashes and harness hang from a hook near the enclosure door. Everything's all set.

Late that afternoon, Lisa and Ella watch Solomon follow the treat trail into the far reaches of the enclosure. To Lisa, he seems much more relaxed eating that far in than he'd seemed even a few days ago.

Is he, finally, about to decide he's found home? That it's time to end his long journey? Lisa decides to call Leslie and revisit Plan B, just in case they need to use it. The thought of driving Solomon out to that canyon in Utah and leaving him at the sanctuary, of the heartbreaking drive back home without him, is nightmarish to Lisa. She can barely contemplate the possibility, let alone discuss it. But they have to.

"I think he may be ready," she tells Leslie. "He's been eating from far back into the enclosure for a while now. I think it may be time to pull the rope."

"Oh my God...I can't believe this may really be coming to an end for him, after all this time. So amazing!"

"I know. And I think it's all going to be fine. But just in case I'm wrong, I think we should go over Plan B."

"I have the same feeling," Leslie says. "Everything's going to be fine, and we're not going to need Plan B. But yeah, just in case we're wrong, let's think it through again and have it all ready to go."

After dinner, Lisa decides to do an equipment check.

"Ella, sweetie, can you come here for a sec?" she calls.

Ella appears in the kitchen doorway, looking expectantly at Lisa.

"Let's test the walkie-talkies, okay?"

"Okay!"

Ella is fascinated by the walkie-talkies, dances happily around the kitchen as her mother retrieves them from the shelf in the broom closet. Lisa lays the walkie-talkies side by side on the counter. She picks one up, examines it, then does the same with the other. Should she replace the batteries? She put fresh batteries in the set the day she bought it, and it wasn't that long ago. Only a package of fluky dud batteries would go dead in such a short time.

Still, she pops open the battery door on each walkie-talkie and empties out what are likely perfectly good batteries, replacing them with new ones. She then switches both Ella's handset and hers into the "On" position.

"Perfect. Let's go see if these work. When I get to my window, I'll yell to you that I'm ready. And then you say the code word, okay? Remember, this little switch has to be pushed over this way for it to work."

Ella nods. "I know, Mommy. You showed me before."

"Just reminding you," Lisa says, bending down to kiss the top of Ella's head.

They take their places, Lisa on the porch, Ella in the dining room.

"Okay, ready," Lisa hollers.

"Solomon," she hears over her walkie-talkie. It's loud and clear, her daughter's voice solemnly repeating their code word.

"I hear you, Ella," she replies. "The walkie-talkies work."

"Now Solly can come live with us!"

"God, let it be," Lisa whispers.

With the walkie-talkies all set, she turns her attention to the rope contraption. It occurs to her that, before testing the rope, it might be good to spray some WD-40 on the enclosure's door latch. That should eliminate any possibility of the latch sticking when she pulls the rope.

"Be back in a few minutes, Ella," she calls. "I'm going outside to check the latch."

She walks down the basement stairs, grabs the WD-40 from the worktable. Standing outside the enclosure door, she jiggles the latch a few times. The cold seems to have had no effect on it. But still. Why take unnecessary chances? Prevention's always better than hindsight. She gives the latch a good blast of WD-40, then jiggles it a few more times. Perfect. That latch won't be freezing up anytime soon.

Back upstairs, she returns to the window and tugs the taut rope upward. She hears the latch click faintly, and goes back outside to check the enclosure door. It's shut, the latch secure. Her simple plan, with its basic equipment, is actually going to work. *If* Solomon wants it to.

It's the first day of December and below freezing in Hull Village, a quarter inch of snow dusting the ground. The Parsons family has just finished breakfast, and Ella is still in her pajamas, curled up on the living room couch watching Saturday morning cartoons. Lisa clears away the dishes and prepares Solomon's food. She has a strong feeling that today might be the day. There's nothing in particular that makes her feel this way. She just does. It would be a good idea, she thinks, for her and Ella to get dressed.

"Ella, let's go upstairs and get dressed. Then we'll go bring Solomon his breakfast and wait for him."

"But my cartoon's not over yet."

Lisa glances at the kitchen clock. Eight more minutes.

"Okay. You can finish watching it, but then it's time to get dressed."

No argument from her daughter.

The music that signals the end of Ella's cartoon filters into the kitchen, and Lisa walks into the living room.

"Ready?"

Ella nods, turns off the tv.

Ten minutes later they're back downstairs in the kitchen. Solomon's food has gotten cold sitting on the counter, and Lisa pops it into the microwave. When the timer beeps, she removes the bowl and places it back on the counter.

"Go put your jacket on," she tells Ella.

When her daughter returns, Lisa pulls the bag of treats out of the cabinet. "Here you go," she says, handing the bag to Ella.

Ella, jacket on but unzipped, takes the bag, smiling with the anticipation of laying down Solomon's treat trail.

"Let's zip you up. It's cold out." Lisa kneels down in front of her daughter and zips her jacket. "Okay, all set. Let's go!"

She throws her own jacket on, then takes the bowl of warm food from the counter. The two of them walk down the basement stairs and out to the enclosure. Lisa points to a spot just a little farther into the space than Solomon has previously gone.

"How 'bout we start the treats from right here?" she asks Ella. Ella begins dropping treats there, working her way across the enclosure, out the door, and into the yard.

Lisa sets Solomon's food down at the spot she pointed out to Ella, then goes back inside and returns with a bowl of water. She hopes he'll arrive for his meal before the water freezes.

"All done, Mommy." Ella comes back into the enclosure, an expression of satisfaction on her face.

"Thank you, sweetheart. Good job! Let's go back inside and get our walkie-talkies ready before Solomon gets here."

Ella runs inside and up the stairs ahead of Lisa, beside herself with excitement. Finally—she's going to get to use the walkie-talkie when she sees Solomon, and Solomon will be coming to live with them! By the time Lisa reaches the top of the stairs, Ella is already at her post.

"Okay, let's practice again. You turn the switch on, like this, then leave it on. Then you talk into it. If you see Solomon right at the food bowl, what are you going to say into the walkie-talkie?"

Ella looks at Lisa in disbelief. Does her mother really think she's forgotten the code word?

"*Solomon.*"

Lisa hears the peeve in Ella's voice. "Sorry, Ella. I know you remember. I'm just really nervous and want to make sure nothing goes wrong. Okay, let's try the walkie-talkies one more time, make sure they work."

Leaving the room, Lisa walks into the kitchen. "Ella, can you hear me?" she asks into the device.

"Yup. Can you hear me?"

"I can!"

Everything is working. Now it's just a matter of waiting for Solomon. She can't ask a six-year-old to spend Saturday sitting by a window, so she plans to give it an hour. If Solomon isn't standing inside the enclosure by then, there's always the dinner feeding.

Solomon plods through the soft sand of the small bayside beach. He usually finds it warmer than the oceanside beach, but today he shivers as he does his business in the brittle shelter of the dried-out dune grass. He leaves the beach and heads back to his neighborhood, the warmth of movement coursing pleasurably through his body.

The neighborhood feels comfortably familiar to him now. He moves through it confidently, unafraid of allowing himself to be seen. He has everything he needs: food, water, shelter. Places to play, and places to hide out when he wants to. Still, there's something missing, the absence of which he senses acutely.

Since the day he stood on the porch looking in at the humans, he's felt the loneliness of being a solitary pack animal. It's a loneliness he sometimes expresses in hollow, heartbreaking howls that puncture the silence of the wee hours.

He has never before wanted to live with humans. But these humans feel different to him. He's grown to trust them, to rely on them for his food, his water. Scent clues tell him they're the source of his toys, his blanket. He senses he'll be accepted into their pack. And he has seen a kindness within it that he craves.

He stops his brisk trot through the neighborhood directly across the street from the big yellow Victorian. His instincts, so finely honed and accurate from his constant reliance on them for survival, tell him this is where he belongs. This is where his pack is. He is ready, finally, to join it.

They've been in position, by their windows, for nearly half an hour. Every five minutes or so Lisa checks in with Ella on the walkie-talkie. So far, Ella is holding up well. She's usually fine with sitting still, as long as her mind is engaged. And right now she's as engaged as Lisa has ever seen her. Cartoons forgotten, Ella is focused on one thing: her role in helping Solomon come inside to live with her family.

And then he appears. His black and white body is so familiar and beloved to Lisa, she could describe its patterning with her eyes closed. He trots confidently across the yard, head up and tail high, in the direction of the enclosure for the day's first meal.

"Ella, here comes Solomon," she says into the walkie-talkie. "Keep your eyes on your spot."

"I will, Mommy."

Solomon slows down, his nose detecting the beginning of the treat trail. He gobbles up the first few treats eagerly. Meandering the rest of the way to the enclosure, head zig-zagging through the grass, he finds and devours every last treat. At the enclosure door he enters without hesitation. He stands for a few seconds, eyes adjusting to the change in light. Then he moves farther into the space, around a corner, and into a slightly smaller area. He sees the bowls, smells the food. The meat is mixed with kibble, and he takes his time chewing and crunching.

Lisa can't see Solomon now, but knows Ella can. Lisa's heart thumps against the wall of her chest. "We're so close," she whispers. Is it really going to end today, this long, strange journey that's brought them together? Her senses are heightened, every sound magnified, every pore electrified. When the word comes over the walkie-talkie, her tightly wound body startles at the sound of it.

"Solomon!"

She lifts the sill and pulls upward on the rope. They're the same actions she's rehearsed in her mind several times a day for the past five weeks. But this time, they're for real. She's sure she heard the latch click. But is he still inside? Or did he hear the closing door scraping the dirt floor and manage to slip out, not quite ready to stay? She calls Ella on the walkie-talkie.

"Is he still there, sweetie? Can you see him?"

"I see him. He's eating his food."

So he hadn't raced out the door before it closed.

"How about now? Can you see him now?"

"No, I can't see him anymore."

If Ella can't see him, that means he's in the outer part of the enclosure, probably standing by the door. She knows they need to get down there, before he has a chance to feel trapped or to panic.

"Let's go see if Solomon's inside."

Ella jumps up from her chair and races across the room, beating Lisa to the kitchen.

Opening the door leading from the kitchen to the basement stairs, Lisa turns to Ella.

"I know we're excited. But we need to be quiet going down the stairs. And especially quiet when we see Solomon, so we don't scare him."

Ella nods, her expression serious.

"Close the door tight behind you before you come down the stairs, okay? We don't want Solomon to meet the cats yet."

With Ella a few steps behind, Lisa hurries down the basement stairs. She stops briefly to grab the two brand-new leashes from their hook, and then, body trembling, opens the door.

🐕

Solomon stands at the enclosure door, his exit blocked. Surprised, he sniffs around the base of the door. Nothing out of the ordinary. No new or out-of-place scents. He paws at the side of the door, gently at first, then vigorously. He can see the outside through the door's small spaces, but can't get there.

Solomon hears footsteps on the other side of the wall, and turns in their direction. A door opens, and standing on the other side are two figures. He recognizes them by sight and smell. They're the humans he saw through the window, the humans who leave his food and water, his treats and toys. They're the humans who are his pack.

Despite this recognition his body shivers, involuntary waves of anxiety rippling over his skin, contracting his muscles and tendons. Out of habit he wants to run, to hide, but stands rooted in place as the humans slowly approach. Suddenly, they stop. He watches as they lower themselves to the ground, becoming closer to his own size. Their eyes turn away from his, a gesture of non-aggression. For a short time, there is silence. Then he hears the familiar, soothing voice, the voice he associates with food and comfort.

"Hi, Solomon."

The humans stand again, calmly. The larger human, the one he understands to be the alpha, moves slowly in his direction. His keen eyes observe her shaking body, his discriminating sense of smell catches the scent of something close to fear.

And so when she again lowers herself to his height, and her hand reaches out to touch the side of his neck, he allows it to remain there. He stands quietly, the hand moving from his neck to his head and back down his neck. The touch is soft, gentle, and he feels its kindness all the way to his core. For the first time in his life, Solomon knows he is where he belongs. There is nothing to fear, no need to run. After so much time alone, after so many miles traveled, he's finally found his way home.

Lisa continues running her hand along Solomon's head and neck. That he allows her to do so makes her heart feel such joy. The leashes she grabbed on her way out into the enclosure dangle around her neck in a way she hopes is nonthreatening. Finally, she stops petting him. She reaches out to touch his battered, dirt-crusted collar before clipping the two leashes onto the D-ring. She rises slowly, then places her hand lightly on the ridge of Solomon's neck.

"C'mon, Solomon. Let's go home."

And then, like it's the most natural thing in the world, he walks unhesitatingly along beside his new family into the warmth and safety of the basement. Just as if it was always meant to be, as if he'd always known.

Twenty

The ease with which Solomon followed her and Ella inside astounds Lisa, and probably always will. So much time on his own, so many escapes, so many failed attempts to recover him. How was it this easy? Is he really sitting on his brand-new bed in her warm basement, letting her and Ella pet him?

Yes, he is.

Lisa wonders what to do next. Should they go upstairs and leave him alone for a while? Or will that make him anxious, given the unfamiliarity of his new environment? She decides to leave him alone just long enough to go upstairs and make some hot chocolate.

"C'mon, sweetie, let's go make some hot chocolate. We'll bring it back down here and drink it, keep Solomon company."

"Okay. Is Solomon going to come upstairs with us after that?"

"Not yet. He needs a little time to get used to his new home before he meets the cats."

"How much time?" Ella asks.

"Well, I don't know. Maybe a week or two?"

"A week? Or *two*?"

"Solomon's been by himself for a long, long time," she says, stroking Ella's head. "He needs a while to get used to living inside, and to being with people again. He'll be upstairs with us soon."

Ella sighs. "Okay. Let's go make our chocolate."

Back upstairs in the kitchen Lisa pours the hot chocolate, shoots an extra blast of whipped cream into Ella's, then picks up both mugs.

"Can you grab my cell phone from the island, and then open the door to the basement? And before you come down the stairs make sure you shut the door really tight behind you. I want to hear it!"

Lisa and Ella head down the stairs, over to where Solomon sits on his bed watching them approach. They lower themselves onto the cement floor near his bed. Close, but still giving him his space. Sipping her chocolate, Lisa gazes at Solomon, her emotions ricocheting wildly. Love, hope, admiration, awe. She finds reassurance in his journey, a belief that her own search for the person she truly belongs with will also end happily.

But there's also worry in her caroming emotions. The worry of wondering if Solomon is healthy. If he'll be able to adjust to a life indoors with a family, with cats. After an hour of sitting with Solomon and her thoughts, she picks up the phone and calls Leslie.

"Leslie?"

"Lisa, hey! What's going on?"

"Are you sitting down? Ella and I are. On the basement floor. And guess who's sitting about seven feet away? On his very own brand-new bed, looking at us?"

Leslie plops onto her couch as quickly as if someone had buckled the back of her knees.

"Oh my God. Are you serious? *Solomon?*"

"Yes!"

"How'd you get him inside?"

Lisa recounts how Solomon had gone inside the far section of the enclosure to eat, Ella had given the code word, and Lisa had pulled the rope, latching the door. How she and Ella had approached Solomon, gotten down to his level with no eye contact. How eventually, very slowly, she'd reached out and hooked the recommended two leashes onto his old collar.

"And then I said 'C'mon, Solomon … let's go home,' and he walked right in beside us. Like he'd known us all his life."

Leslie sits with that for a moment, letting it all sink in.

"So he's fine with Ella?"

"She's right here with me, sitting not too far from Solomon's bed, and he's totally fine with her. I think he's reassured by her size, actually."

"What about the cats? Has he seen them yet?"

"No. I think it's too soon for that."

Leslie agrees. A couple of weeks, give or take, depending on how things go. Neither woman mentions Plan B.

"I still can't believe he finally decided it was time to come inside," Leslie says.

"I know. Even though I'm sitting here looking at him it still feels surreal. Like a dream."

"So what's next?" Leslie asks.

"Well, I always assumed I'd take him to the vet right away, get him checked out. But now, I don't know. I think it might be too traumatic for him. But maybe I should? It's hard to know what's the best thing for him. If you're not too busy, would you mind coming over to just, you know, take a look at him? And then we can take it from there?"

"Do I *mind*? I thought you'd never ask!"

Lisa laughs, releasing the tension she hadn't realized her shoulders were holding.

"Thanks, Leslie. See you soon."

🐕

While she waits for Leslie, Lisa watches Ella and Solomon. Children and animals. They're similar in so many ways, she thinks. Especially the way they never let the mind cloud or clutter the heart's truths.

"Solly." Ella reaches out to touch Solomon without the slightest fear or hesitation. She strokes his head gently. "I love you, Solomon."

The tenderness in Ella's voice, the look of absolute trust in Solomon's eyes as he gazes at her, confirm what Lisa has always believed. Ella and Solomon are going to be the best of friends, emotional anchors for each other as they go through life together. Lisa's marriage will end, Ella's family situation will change. But Solomon will be there, his love unconditional, as solid as a rock.

On the way over to Lisa's, Leslie reflects back to an incident from months ago, the images powerful enough to have retained their original detail and clarity. It was the day she and Lisa had been sitting on Lisa's porch steps talking, the day Lisa had said, "I want him." And as soon as she'd said it, Solomon had appeared from the bushes and walked right by, really slowly. Like he wanted to let them know he'd heard them, that he was down with it. She'd been convinced right then that if Solomon ever decided to live with people, it would be with this family and only this family. And it would be on his own terms, when he was ready.

Which is exactly how it all happened in the end. Yes, he was secured inside the enclosure by a rigged door. But it was his choice all along to trust, to eat from that far inside the space. He didn't have to; he was more than adept at finding his own food. He *chose* to. Leslie is convinced that the Parsons family is Solomon's destiny, the entire point of his improbable journey through New England.

She also thinks he's known it all along. Not in a thought-out, human way of knowing, but instinctively. The homes he'd been in weren't where he belonged, and despite easy access to food, water, warmth, and care, he ran from them. Then he arrives in Hull Village, where he has minimal comforts and necessities. Where he knows people are trying to catch him. And yet he stays. Why? Because he knows, somehow, that this is where he belongs. It's the only reason that makes sense to her.

Would she ever have believed something like this before becoming involved in the effort to recover Solomon? No way. But she believes it now, no questions asked. She knows her experience with Solomon will forever change the way she thinks about missing dogs. Not every missing dog is lost. She makes a promise to herself, and to Solomon, to never forget that lesson.

Lisa is waiting for Leslie in the kitchen when she arrives. Dave, now back from checking out the progress on the house renovations, is downstairs sitting with Ella and Solomon.

"C'mon down and see the magnificent Solomon," Lisa says, leading the way down the stairs into the basement. "Make sure the door's closed behind you."

Leslie pulls the door shut, then grabs the doorknob, rattles the door back and forth. That door's going nowhere.

She follows Lisa into the basement and there he is, staring at them from his dog bed.

"Hey, handsome," Leslie says softly. "Welcome home."

She and Lisa sit down next to Ella on the floor. Leslie tries not to make eye contact with Solomon. For a dog living outside on his own just a couple of hours ago, he seems to be adjusting to his new surroundings with a surprising calm. If this is Solomon at the beginning of hour three, by the time a week passes he should be doing just fine.

"What do you think?" Lisa asks. "Does he look okay to you, or do you think we should take him to the vet?"

From the outside he looks great. His coat shines, and he's at a healthy weight thanks to the protein-rich meals Lisa has been making for him twice a day. Leslie can't see any cuts or other injuries to his torso or limbs. It's hard to say what's going on inside him, though. He's been living outside for ten months since his last escape, through the summer with dog ticks and deer ticks and the kamikaze Hull Village mosquitos. It's highly likely he has a tick-borne disease, or heartworm, or both.

"He looks good physically. But there could definitely be stuff going on inside. He needs to be checked out, for sure, but I think it's fine to wait a few days."

Lisa is reassured by Leslie's assessment. She wants to give Solomon every chance to be his best self with strangers. Bringing him to the vet on his first day inside probably isn't going to accomplish that.

"That's what I was hoping you'd say," Lisa tells Leslie. "I think he's been through enough new experiences for one day."

Over the next hour, the two women sit together on the floor discussing what to do in terms of the day-to-day. Leslie thinks it's fine for Lisa to leave Solomon alone for a few hours at a time.

"When you go back down to see him, give him a treat and sit with him for a while. That way he'll learn that when you go away, you always come back. I think you just take the rest of it day by day," she tells Lisa.

Lisa will keep him in the basement for a week, they agree, and then they'll see where he's at and move forward from there.

Solomon's new space is quiet and warm. The humans have left, and he is alone. There's no need to curl into his usual tight ball, to cover his nose with his forelegs and paws to protect it from the cold. He stretches out lengthwise across the soft bed that molds to his shape, and sleeps.

The sights and sounds of his new surroundings still unfamiliar, he's startled awake by a rumbling noise. This is followed by a low, humming sound coming from a corner of the room. Solomon rises from his bed, follows the humming. The source of the sound is a large object he's never seen before. Circling its perimeter cautiously, he gives the object a thorough sniff. Though it radiates warmth from all sides, and makes at least two distinct noises, it's clearly not alive.

His curiosity satisfied, Solomon begins an exploration of the rest of the space. From side to side, end to end, and corner to corner he moves, observing, listening, sniffing. In one area, he detects remnants of a familiar urine scent. It's a scent left by a particular small animal he's occasionally encountered outside. When these animals are frightened, they spit and hiss and make themselves larger. The small animals have definitely been here in his space, but not recently.

Walking back across the basement to his bed, he stops in front of his water bowl. The water is free of bugs and leaves and pine needles, and he drinks enthusiastically. He doesn't feel particularly thirsty; he drinks simply for the pleasure of perfectly clean water.

Everything Lisa's been reading on raising dogs says they're creatures of habit, driven by routine. Establishing a routine to replace the one he had when he was on his own is important. Feeding him on the schedule he's used to will be a good start, she thinks. And then she needs to get him on a going-outside schedule. First thing in the morning, last thing at night, and an hour after eating makes sense to her. Really, though, she has no idea what that particular schedule was in his outdoor life. In the beginning, she's going to have to wing it. Might as well start now.

Walking down the basement stairs with Ella, Lisa calls to him softly, giving advance notice of their approach.

"Hi, Solomon."

"Solomon, want to go out?" Ella asks.

He probably has no idea what that means, Lisa thinks. She doubts he even knows his name. But he's proven himself a fast learner, and she's confident he'll soon come to understand her language. She hopes she'll be an equally quick study when it comes to learning his. Solomon sits calmly on his bed, watching them walk toward him. Lisa's eyes well when she sees the imprint of his shape across the length of the bed. That he feels safe enough in his new home to let down his guard and sleep, all stretched out, moves her deeply.

Lisa walks past him, over to the door leading into the enclosure, and removes the two leashes from their hook. She brings them over to Solomon's bed, then kneels on the floor in front of him. "Okay, Solomon, let's get these on so you can go out to pee."

She reaches over, clips one leash and then the other onto his collar's d-ring. The situation with Solomon's collar, which is not in good condition, is concerning to Lisa. What if he pulls hard when she's walking him and it breaks? She'll be left, horrified, holding two leashes and half a collar. And what if she screams, frightening Solomon and making him run? It would be her worst nightmare, come to life.

But she also thinks it might be too soon to remove his collar and replace it with a new one. The new martingale she bought for him has to be slipped over his head and adjusted. And the old one, which is snug now, needs to be adjusted in order to be removed. She worries that all the tugging at and around his neck as she adjusts the collars might be interpreted as aggression. Better to just take him out into the enclosure where there's no chance of losing him. The cats sometimes do their business out there on the dirt floor. Why can't he?

Pulling the door to the enclosure open, she wonders what he'll do when he smells the outdoors again. Will he pull her toward the enclosure door in an effort to escape? She has no idea.

"Okay, Solomon, go pee."

To her astonishment, he does exactly as he's asked. Maybe he'd been house trained in Georgia before he ended up in the shelter, or maybe Carmen and Steve had trained him. Still, that he remembers this command after two years of relieving himself wherever and whenever he pleased amazes her.

She and Ella walk Solomon around in the enclosure, both for the exercise and to give him time to complete any further business. Back inside, he returns to the comfort, scent, and security of his bed. Lisa and Ella sit on the floor, close to him. Lisa slowly runs her hand along his back, and Ella's smaller hand reaches out alongside her mother's to do the same. He hasn't even been there a full day, but they're as attached to him as if he'd been with them forever. It's all exactly as Lisa had imagined it would be.

Solomon settles into his new routine. The humans take him outside to the enclosure. They come back inside. He eats. Then he sits on his bed. The humans pet him, speak to him. And then they leave. Later they return, and the cycle begins again.

In between these cycles, Solomon spends his time listening. He listens to the noises overhead, to the life not yet accessible to him. A life he can hear but not see, smell but not feel. He learns to distinguish one set of human footsteps from another, the heavier steps from the lighter steps from the steps even lighter than those. When he hears the door open, followed by steps on the basement stairs, his tail wags.

He hears other steps, too. They're not human steps. They're much smaller and lighter, and move in strange ways across the space above him. Sometimes, these steps seem to travel in a straight line. But sometimes they land with heavy thudding sounds that move rapidly, and in many directions. Solomon has no idea why this happens. On the second day of living in his new home, he's curious enough to climb the stairs to learn more about these unusual steps.

Standing at the top of the stairs, Solomon presses his nose against the crack beneath the door. On the other side of the door he smells a scent he recognizes. It belongs to the small animals, the ones he knows have been in his space. He hears a yowling sound, then a scratching at the door. He wedges his nose under the door and sniffs deeply, audibly, trying to make sense of everything using only his ears and nose.

He promptly learns that the small animals on the other side of the door have boundaries he's overstepped. Before he can extricate his nose from the crack he feels a quick whack, accompanied by a hissing sound. More surprised than hurt, he retreats immediately down the stairs to his bed. At least, for now.

Sitting at the kitchen island browsing through the day's mail, Lisa hears the basement steps creak. The creaking is muffled but persistent, then stops. She senses Solomon on the other side of the basement door before she hears him, even before the cats alert her to his presence. That he's curious enough about the sounds he hears from below to venture up the stairs, see what they're all about, is another encouraging sign that he's feeling secure in his new home.

That it's all going to be fine.

She sees the black of his nose poke beneath the crack under the basement door, hears the little huffs of breath. The cats meow and scratch at the door, as curious about him as he is about them. And then, before she can anticipate what's coming, a cat hisses, reaches out a paw, and bats Solomon, hard, on his nose.

She doesn't hear him yelp, so assumes the cat's claws were retracted. A warning, nothing more. Still, she hears Solomon retreat down the stairs. She's sorry his exploration ends in this way.

"No!" Lisa scolds the cats. "That wasn't very nice. That's Solomon. He's our dog, and he's going to live with us from now on."

The cats still sit in front of the basement door, daring the interloper to return. They look up at her, their expressions a mixture of innocence and bewilderment. She feels bad for reprimanding them. Their lives have been turned upside down since she started feeding Solomon in the enclosure. No playing on their indoor–outdoor kitty jungle gym. And now they can't go down to the basement to use their litter boxes, have had to adjust to their bathrooms being elsewhere.

Bending down, she pets them both.

"Never mind, it's okay. You and Solomon will be friends. I promise."

Watching the cats scamper off, Lisa knows she's going to have to introduce them to Solomon very carefully. But as long as she does, she sees no reason why all the Parsons animals won't be able to peacefully co-exist.

It's the morning of Solomon's third full day in her basement, and Lisa thinks he's adjusting well. Still, she'd prefer to wait another few days for this next milestone. But she has a nagging feeling that it's better not to. It's time to take him to the vet.

Or, better yet, for the vet to come to him.

There's a local veterinarian with a mobile practice, and Lisa calls to ask about appointment availability. When the vet hears Solomon's story, she makes time for him later that day. Solomon will be spared the potential trauma of a trip to the vet. Even so, Lisa worries he might react negatively to a stranger touching him, examining his teeth, poking him with needles to draw blood. She calls Leslie.

"Solomon's got an appointment with the mobile vet this afternoon. I know it's short notice, but do you think you could come over?"

"Absolutely. Unless an emergency comes up, I'll be there."

"Thanks, Leslie. See you later."

Leslie's looking forward to the visit. She's been hooked on Solomon from the moment she laid eyes on him. Any chance she has to see him, no matter the circumstances, is irresistible.

The mobile vet is kind and gentle, with a sense of awe for all that Solomon has been through. Solomon stands near his bed calmly, sensing the good intentions of the woman who kneels on the floor beside him.

"What a handsome boy you are. And so intelligent. You've traveled a long, long way to find your home, haven't you?"

She runs her hand softly over his head, his spine, her voice a low coo.

"Okay, here we go. I'm just going to look at your beautiful teeth. Good boy."

Solomon stands quietly, one of his humans kneeling protectively by his side, another human he recognizes sitting beside her. The vet puts something cold against his heart and listens. She runs her hands along his side, his belly, pressing lightly, then lifts his forelegs, bends his joints.

"He looks great," the vet says. "He's obviously eaten well since he landed in Hull Village, and his weight's right where it should be. I'll run a fecal, but I'm really not worried about his having worms."

Lisa smiles. "Well, that's good news."

"It is, definitely. What I *am* worried about is the possibility of a tick-borne disease like Lyme or ehrlichiosis. And obviously, with the mosquito problem down here, heartworm. Given his history, a heartworm diagnosis would be particularly unfortunate because his heart and lungs were almost certainly compromised from his first go-round with it."

"Could he have both Lyme and heartworm?" Lisa asks. That, she thinks, would be the ultimate tragedy. Finally welcoming Solomon into her family, only to have him die.

"Yes, but let's not get ahead of ourselves." The vet smiles kindly at Lisa. "I'm going to need to get some blood from him, which I hope he'll let me do. And then we should know by early next week if there's anything going on."

"Okay."

"So, I think the best way to get his blood will be to have him sit. Then if you can distract him by petting him, maybe he'll let me get the tourniquet on and take his blood."

"What if he won't?"

"Then we'll try again in another couple of days, after he's had more time to adjust. I'm happy to come back as many times as it takes, given his circumstances."

Lisa has no idea if anyone has ever taught him commands, but she'll find out now.

"Solomon, sit." Lisa's voice is encouraging, but he remains standing, tail tucked.

"Sit," she says again, pushing lightly downward on his rump.

He sits, tentatively, rump not quite firmly on the floor. Lisa can see he's nervous, but he clearly wants to please. So maybe someone *has* taught him commands, she thinks. She wonders what else he knows.

"Good boy," Lisa says. She gives him a few scratches behind his ears.

"Okay, perfect," the vet says. "Good boy, Solomon. Can you give me your paw?"

She picks up his right front paw. Solomon licks his lips, but allows her to hold his paw loosely in her hand.

"Good boy. Now I'm going to tie this little piece of rubber around your leg, get some blood, and we'll be all set." She looks over at Lisa and Leslie. "Okay, distract him if you can."

Lisa runs her hand along Solomon's head and back, feels his body flinch slightly as the needle enters his vein. The syringe begins to fill with red.

"That's it," the vet says. "I've got all I need."

She removes the needle, places a patch of gauze over the tiny puncture. Lisa and Leslie look at each other, smiling. Solomon's biggest test so far is over, and he didn't just pass it. He aced it.

The vet begins packing up, and Solomon retreats to the safety of his bed.

"You've got a really amazing dog there," the vet tells Lisa. "To be this good with a complete stranger poking him with a needle, after being outside on his own for two years? It's incredible."

"Thank you," Lisa replies. "We think he's pretty special, and we're so grateful he chose us as his family."

"I'm sure he's grateful, too. Never think dogs don't feel gratitude. They definitely do. I'll be in touch as soon as the test results are in."

The following Tuesday, Lisa's phone rings. She reads the caller ID. It's the vet.

"Hello?" Her voice is tight, strained.

"Hi, Lisa. I've got the results in from Solomon's bloodwork."

Lisa grips the phone hard, listening.

"Are you sure? Are you absolutely sure?"

"Yes, I'm sure."

"Can the tests be wrong?"

"It's possible. But not in this case. Lyme tests can give a false negative, but a positive result's always accurate. And with the heartworm test I used, which is the most highly-rated one out there, false positives can happen, but not false negative. So Solomon's negative test is right."

"So he's definitely positive for Lyme, but negative for heartworm."

"Yes, amazingly. Then again, I think this dog has traveled through life blessed, so maybe it's not so amazing after all."

Lyme is treatable with doxycycline, and Lisa provides the vet with her pharmacy's phone number to call in the prescription.

"It might upset his stomach or give him some diarrhea. Keep an eye on him, and let me know if he's not reacting well to it."

Lyme disease isn't something to be taken lightly, and Lisa knows this. Heartworm, though, is terrifying. She's done some research on the treatment for heartworm, the damage caused by the disease. That Solomon doesn't have it again makes the diagnosis of Lyme seem so much less upsetting than it would have been without that reference point.

Lisa calls Leslie immediately after her conversation with the vet.

"I just got Solomon's test results back."

"And?"

"Positive for Lyme, but that's it. His liver and kidney functions are perfect, and he's negative for worms and heartworm. I still can't believe it!"

The negative heartworm result, Leslie thinks, is stunning, its irony impossible to ignore: it was a positive heartworm test that set Solomon's Underhound Railroad journey in motion down in Georgia three Octobers ago. And now that he's found his way to where he belongs? The test is negative. She smiles as sudden chills run up and down her arms, spread into her upper back and neck.

"I can," Leslie says. "He finally found his family, his home. No way was a measly mosquito going to end his life. Not now. Not when the life he was meant to live all along is just beginning."

Twenty-One

The day after getting the blood results, Lisa starts Solomon on his Lyme medication. She notes his appetite, visually examines his stool, and everything looks normal. Life is good. There's still one major test, though, one last hurdle for Solomon to clear: the cats. He's been coming up the basement stairs multiple time a day, standing on the other side of the door, listening. She's watched him stick his nose, curious, under the crack when he knows the cats aren't on the other side. He's ready, she thinks. The basement's been a safe haven, a contained space for him to adjust to living inside. But he wants to be upstairs now, with his family.

Lisa rummages through the hallway closet, looking for the baby gate they used years ago when Ella started crawling. She remembers it being in the closet, but it's not there now. Maybe it got moved down into the basement. Walking down the creaky wooden stairs, she hears the swishing of Solomon's tail against his bed.

"Hi, Solomon!" she says.

She sits beside him on his bed, kisses his head. She loves the way his head smells. The combination of sweet and earthy reminds her of the way a toddler's head smells. Ella still smells that way sometimes; a scent of fresh air, sunlight, and her own body's unique chemistry. Lisa smiles thinking of Ella, believes Solomon feels a special connection to her. It's usually her presence in the kitchen, the sound of her voice and footsteps, that draw him to the top of the stairs. But the cats are a potentially different story.

Lisa gets up and begins searching for the baby gate again. A conservative introduction between Solomon and the cats is the only way to go here. She's either going to find that baby gate or go out and buy a new one. Eventually, she sees a small section of the gate's white plastic lattice jutting out from behind some plywood leaning against the wall. She pulls the gate out, turns it from side to side, inspecting the plastic for breakage.

"A little dusty, but it'll do," she tells Solomon.

Back upstairs, she adjusts the gate's width to fit tightly in the doorway between the kitchen and dining room. Solomon will stay in the kitchen with her, on-leash. Ella and the cats will be on the other side of the gate in the dining room. And then, they'll see what happens. She stands for a moment in the kitchen, envisioning the way she hopes things will go. *All will be well.* She repeats the mantra silently until she becomes lost within it, her breath matched to its rhythm. *All will be well.*

"Solomon," Lisa calls as she walks down the stairs.

He jumps up from his bed and walks over to greet her, tail wagging.

"We're going to go upstairs so you can meet the cats. And in honor of that, we're going to put your new collar on."

The collar, untouched since the day she bought it, is on the worktable. She picks it up, eyeballs Solomon's neck, then adjusts the size and slips it over his head, right below his old collar. It's still loose, but one more adjustment and it fits perfectly. Her eyes fill. The sight of those two collars around his neck, the old and the new, triggers an emotional reaction she hadn't expected. The new collar's vivid red stands out, bright against the white of his neck. For the first time since she's known him, Solomon fully looks the part of a dog who's loved and cared for.

Lisa loosens the old, beat-up collar, then tugs it off over his head. When she looks closely at the inside, she sees a faded reddish hue through the layers of dirt and accumulated white fur. His original martingale collar, which she'd always thought was brown, is actually, like his brand-new one, red. She places it gently on the worktable. That collar is a part of him. Each ripple and crack, each bit of caked earth, frozen water, and faded color, is a testament to the many miles traveled to find her family. *His* family. She intends to save it, in a special place, just as it is.

"Okay, handsome boy. All set," she tells him. Then she clips one of his leashes onto his new collar, and they ascend the basement stairs. When she reaches the top, she opens the door.

"Ella, here we come! Go get the cats and come stand by the gate."

She hears Ella's light footsteps, running from room to room, rounding up the cats.

"Please let this go well," she prays under her breath, refusing to let herself imagine the consequences if it doesn't.

Solomon stands at the top of the stairs beside the human. The dark, immovable object normally blocking his way suddenly opens to light. He walks into the place he's smelled but never seen, the place with the scents of food, the small animals, and his humans. He explores the area thoroughly, sniffing at the baseboards and floor, the furniture and cabinets. This is, he knows, the place where food comes from. The scent of it is everywhere, overpowering the human and animal scents.

His exploration of the area complete, Solomon continues forward, tugging slightly on his leash. In front of him is an object blocking his path into the next space. It's not like the other barrier, the one he sniffs under. This one is small, and he can see right through it. The human walks him over to the barrier. On the other side he sees the little human and the small animals.

The small animals stand together, watching him. He watches them back, calmly, curiously. They make no noise this time, though his senses tell him they're on guard. He stands at a polite distance from the barrier, observing their faces.

The small human reaches out to him over the barrier, and the gentle weight of her touch on his head relaxes him. His tail moves rapidly back and forth.

"Hi, Solly. These are the cats! Do you like them?" Her voice is upbeat as she continues moving her hand along his head.

After a time, he and the other human turn around, go back down the stairs. When they reach the bottom, the human stops. She kneels, arm draped over his back, and pulls him close.

"You're such a good boy, Solomon. I'm so proud of you."

Then his leash is unhooked, and he's free to roam about his space. He stands on his bed, grabs one of his toys. He tosses the gray squirrel into the air. When it falls he grabs it again, jaws it around the middle. It squeaks loudly, and he tosses it again. He's still tossing and catching his toy when the human climbs the stairs and, for a time, disappears.

The success of the first introduction between Solomon and the cats has Lisa on an emotional high. It had all been so civilized. No lunging, no barking or hissing. Really, it was better than she'd dared hope. What she needs to do now, she thinks, is reinforce their reaction to one another; normalize Solomon's presence for the cats, and vice versa.

There's a technique she's recently read about, a method to help new and current animals in a family associate the scent of one another with their humans, accelerating the acceptance process. It breaks her heart that Solomon's still in the basement, listening to his family's life going on without him. If the technique might speed up the process of integrating her animals, why not give it a try right now?

Lisa goes off in search of the cats, finds them lying on either end of the living room sofa. She scoops one of them up and holds her tightly against her chest. When she's sure the cat has smelled Solomon's scent on her, she picks up the other cat, does the same. Then, with the cats' scent all over her, she goes back down the stairs into the basement.

Solomon's playing tires him. He lies on his bed with the squirrel beside him, the toy damp with saliva, its fur sticking up like tiny peaks of meringue. The human walks over to his bed, and he sits up to greet her. Immediately, he notices it. A different smell, a scent like a cross between a human and the small animals. He sniffs and sniffs, the smells mingling together until he associates them all with the human he trusts.

"Want to go out, Solomon?"

He rises, walks out into the enclosure on his two leashes. Through the lattice he sees the yard, and feels a sudden urge to be outside again. To go wherever he wants, to experience the sensory stimulation of ever-changing scents. But his new space is warm and dry and safe. And he's attached to the humans. Especially the smallest one. He turns, leaving the outside behind, and returns to the warmth.

Back inside, the human runs her hand over his head and speaks to him. He recognizes one word in particular, a word he's heard many times: "Solomon."

She turns to leave, and he watches her walk across the room. Soon she'll walk up the stairs and disappear. Just as he has his routine, the human has hers. But instead she stops, turns. She walks back toward him, then squats down to his level. This is not the routine.

"Solomon, come!"

Curious, and happy she's still there, he walks over to her. She presses her body tightly against his.

"Good boy, Solomon. Good boy!"

Solomon understands from the tone of the human's voice that she's happy. He has no idea why she's happy, but wags his tail anyway.

The cat visits are now a regular thing. Usually, Solomon watches the cats through the gate until they get tired of watching him back. Then he hangs around upstairs in the kitchen for a while with Lisa and Ella. On this day, as Lisa moves around the kitchen, she glances over at her daughter and Solomon. The love between the two of them grows daily. She reads it in their faces, in Ella's smile and look of contentment, in Solomon's eyes and the thump of his tail.

Not that she needs these visual confirmations. The happiness they experience in each other's company is palpable enough to feel with her eyes closed, her back turned. They're like magnets, she thinks, pulled together by some invisible energy. The sight of Ella makes Solomon's tail wag like a crazy whirligig, and Ella dances with joy when she sees him. It's time for Solomon to come upstairs and take his place in the family. One more day, she decides. One more day, and that will be it.

"Breathe," Lisa reminds herself. "Breathe."

As she and Solomon climb the basement stairs into the kitchen, she repeats the word silently with each step. It's been a week since Solomon came inside, and she's still amazed at how quickly he's adjusted to his new home. Today is his final milestone. This is it. The moment that will determine everything.

What will happen when there's no gate separating Solomon and the cats? She doesn't know. And what she needs to know, beyond any doubt, is that he won't harm them. That he won't snap, no matter the circumstance. He's given her every reason to believe he won't. Still, her hands shake as she removes the gate from its place in the kitchen doorway. She leans the gate against the wall, then walks with Solomon, still on-leash, into the spacious dining room.

Ella runs across the room to greet him.

"Solly!" She throws her arms around his neck, lays her head against his.

"You're the best, best boy, Solomon," she says. She looks directly into his face as she speaks. Lisa watches Solomon listening to Ella, sees the expression on his face change when Ella says "Solomon." And though Lisa will never be able to know for sure, she'll always believe this to be the moment when he finally understands that the word he's heard for so long, "Solomon," means him.

Through the dining room, into the living room, along the enclosed porch they walk, Solomon sniffing all the way. Then into the den. Lisa wonders if it looks familiar to him, if he remembers it from the time he stood outside, looking in.

One of the cats, Angie, is curled up in a sun spot on the couch. She glances at Solomon with vague interest, but makes no move to bolt from her napping place. Lisa has gotten the cats accustomed to Solomon's scent in the same way she's gotten him used to theirs. Now, apparently, coming into contact with each other's scent is old hat. Everyone belongs, no one is an interloper. Solomon looks at Angie briefly, and that's that. Yes, he's still on-leash, but he doesn't even tug in Angie's direction. Lisa finally knows, with absolute certainty, that Solomon will be staying right where he is.

There'll be no drive out to Utah, no need for Solomon to live out his life in a sanctuary. And now that it's all settled she's ready to go public. The fact that Solomon is living inside with his new family hasn't been a difficult secret for her to keep. It's the way it had to be, until she was sure things were going to work out. But now Lisa wants everyone who's been a part of Solomon's journey to know he's safe, that her home will be his last stop. She texts Beth and Hope, wanting them to be the first to know that although Solomon definitely took the long way home, he has finally and forever come in from the cold.

Beth stares at the text on her phone screen, reading the words again and again. It's from Lisa, and it's the best thing she's read in months, quite possibly all year. The text is accompanied by a photo of Solomon standing in Lisa's basement. Her eyes fill. Finally, unbelievably, Solomon is inside and safe. The text comes out of left field, and if it weren't for the picture, she probably wouldn't believe it. But there he is, living proof that miracles do happen. And perhaps the most amazing thing is that he actually looks happy. Which is, as far as Beth knows, a first when it comes to living indoors with people. Maybe, she thinks, he really *had* known what he was looking for all along. She sits down at her laptop and writes a posting for the GSDR Facebook page, elated to share the final chapter of Solomon's journey with everyone who's followed it.

On December 7, 2012, Hope receives a text and photo from Lisa that make her cry some of the happiest tears she's ever cried. When her emotions settle, she opens the "Help-us-find-Solomon" Facebook page and updates the profile picture. The updated picture is comprised of four photos laid out side by side, comic-strip style. They're from a new GSDR Facebook post titled "Solomon: What a long strange journey: Kittery, Maine 2010 – Hull, Mass 2012." Hope thinks using them as Solomon's new profile picture is the best possible way to announce the safe end of his travels.

In the first picture, a thin, depressed, frightened dog crouches in a shelter run. The caption below the picture reads "In the Shelter, GA." The second photo shows a heavier dog, ears pointed sideways, standing stoically in a snow-covered yard. Its caption reads "Kittery, ME: Dec. 2010." In the third picture, Solomon looks at the photographer from inside a trap. At first glance he appears to be smiling at the person taking his picture. But to a more trained eye, his smile is a nervous pant. The caption for this photo: "Haverhill, MA: Dec. 2011." The final photograph is of Solomon standing in what looks to be a basement. His ears are up, and he looks at something off to the side, his expression curious. "Hull, MA: Dec. 2012."

December seems to be Solomon's month, Hope thinks. It's the month he began living with Carmen and Steve, and the month he exited their home. It's the month he was trapped at Covanta. And now, it's the month he walks into his new home, his new life. It's also the month Hope formally signs his adoption papers. With a few strokes of a pen, Solomon no longer belongs to Underhound Railroad. He's a Parsons now, and he has the papers to prove it.

Solomon, wearing a royal blue-harness, leaps in the snow, ears up and tail high, invigorated by the tiny particles of coldness swirling around his face. He prances and play-postures, waiting for the fun of what he knows comes next. Beside him, Lisa and Ella sit on a sled at the top of a hill, bundled in jackets and snow pants, Dave standing behind them. Lisa pulls the loops of Solomon's leashes over her hand, then wraps her fist tightly around them.

"Okay, Dave—push us off!"

They race down the hill together, Lisa and Ella on the sled, Solomon keeping pace alongside them, breaking his own path through the snow. When they arrive at the bottom, Ella and Lisa roll off the sled, shrieking with laughter. Solomon barks and leaps and wags his tail. And then they all make their way back up through the snow to the top of the hill, and do it all over again.

Epilogue

Lisa sits at the dining room table. The green smell of late May floats through the open window as she scrolls through hundreds of recent photographs on her laptop. She plans to post an update on the "Help-us-find-Solomon" Facebook page, and wants to include photos. But she's finding it difficult to choose the ones most representative of Solomon's life. Finally, she settles on three.

The first is of Solomon standing at the water's edge beneath a pier, the white on his body incandescent in the bright spring sun. The second photo shows him at the end of a very long leash, swimming in shallow, clear water. The last one is of Solomon and Ella in the living room. Solomon is lying on the couch, Ella kneeling on the floor in front of him. Their arms are wrapped tightly around each other's neck, their faces turned toward the camera. It's one of Lisa's favorite pictures of them.

Pictures chosen, she begins to write.

"I just wanted you to know that Solomon is doing wonderful! He is soooo happy and such a perfect family dog. I was walking him today and one of our neighbors came out of the house and said he just couldn't believe that he is the same dog! He is really the sweetest dog I have ever met and he is not only madly in love with my daughter, but he LOVES all the kids in the neighborhood! We often take walks around the time the kids are waiting outside for the bus and he has to go say hello to every one of them! He also is

still great with my cats and actually snuggles with one of them—they really love each other. He still loves the beach and now that it is warm out, he goes swimming almost every day (on the extension leash, now 26' extension!). Photos are attached of Solomon "hugging" his girl, Solomon swimming, and Solomon looking happy at the beach."

The comments on her post start popping up almost immediately. Some are from people who followed Solomon's story from the beginning. Others are from people who hung flyers for him, spent long hours looking for him, prayed for him. They'd all wanted nothing less than the happiest of endings for him. And that's exactly what he got. Lisa is touched by their comments, grateful that he still holds such a special place in their hearts.

"Solomon is near and dear to my heart. I volunteer for GSDR and followed Solomon from Haverhill to Stoughton to Hull. Thank you for these beautiful photos."

"I think Solomon did what he did so that he could end up where he wanted to be..."

"This dog spent a long time just searching for his perfect home, so glad he finally found you!"

"What a beautiful sight!"

"A match made in heaven."

"This warms my heart. So awesome!"

"I'm so happy!!! This warms my heart like crazy. Years of looking for this little loner. So happy he found his peeps..."

"Such a love story. I would have never believed that it would end like this. What a miracle."

It really *is* something of a miracle, Lisa thinks. Solomon's story clearly resonates with so many wonderful people, people whose own stories she'll never know. And though she feels a connection to each of them, she can't help but hope that Solomon's journey speaks most deeply to the ones who were once, like her, lost or adrift, but still believed, with their whole hearts, in the power of love and destiny to guide them home.

Acknowledgments

I am deeply indebted to the following people:

My agent Janet Reid, for supporting a different path for this book than we'd envisioned.

Colin Rolfe and the team at Epigraph Publishing Service, for their design work and truly stellar author support.

My talented and infinitely patient cover designer Ann Kirchner, who got it just right.

Simone Payment, whose insightful editorial suggestions made the book better.

For helping me connect the pieces of Solomon's story by generously sharing their part of it with me, I'm eternally grateful to Ronda Avila, Leslie Badger, Lori Bertrand, Beth Corr, Hope Cruser, Sheila D'Arpino, Carmen Fernandez, Liz Palmer, Bob Spinney, Bella Travaglini, Lisa Vaillancourt, and Irene Williams.

Marisel Pérez and Coco, you are my home.

Finally, my profoundest gratitude to Lisa Parsons and Ella Parsons for opening their home to me, answering my many questions, showing me around Hull Village and visiting some of Solomon's haunts, and most especially for allowing me to share Solomon's amazing, uplifting story in the pages of this book.

About the Author

Gail Gilmore has logged many, many hours walking the woods and cruising the streets as a field volunteer for Missing Dogs Massachusetts. She is the author of *Dog Church*, a memoir about love, change, and learning to let go. Currently, she is working on her first novel. She lives in New Hampshire with her spouse and their rescue dog, Coco.